'Animals h᷉ ... ... ure span of
many thousa ... ... that of the average
the average c ... ...
human bein᷉ ... ᴜkely therefore that within the
animal kingdom there are change management, growth
and adaptive instincts. Cathy deVrye has used her
incisive mind to identify a few pointers of interest
from our zoological friends and to publish them as an
amusing pot pourri of characteristics that good
managers may well take to heart.'

Tony Jollye
Australian Institute of Management

'The commonsense approach to leadership is an
approach Catherine has taken over many years in her
successful career. She has helped me to inculcate this
same thought, leadership, and caring work
environment into our team at American Express
Business Travel Australia. This book is an excellent
reference for those leaders working toward achieving
the same consistent, thoughtful leadership necessary
for today's demanding work life.'

Les Galbraith
Vice President
American Express Business Travel
Australia & New Zealand

'An incredibly innovative and effective way for
executive managers to quickly understand and retain
essential elements of client service.'

Ben Dalton
Former Manager, Client Service Development Program
Queensland Treasury

'At times I have the impression that commercial society marches further and further into a service wilderness—a landscape of undefined standards, insincere attempts and 'that'll do' traps. Cathy's approach to stimulate positive attitudes for excellent customer service by considering a 'walk through the zoo' is original as well as effective.'

Peter Wiesner
Manager, Advertising and Sales Promotion
Mercedes-Benz (Australia) Pty Ltd

'. . . a lively jargon-free short read that will give long-term benefits in improving the quality of service in an organisation . . . timely and relevant!'

Liz Burrows
Qualty Assurance Manager
Blackmores Ltd

'A quick 'must read' for all executives who think they understand customer service. The analogies at first seem simple, but Cathy has produced a very sound, up-to-date, instructional tool on the service ethic.'

Dr Vern Harvey
Chief Executive
Credit Union Services Corporation

'To be successful in business you must know the importance of customer service. To anyone wanting an edge on their competitor, I recommend this book, written in an effective and entertaining way, highlighting the key elements of good customer service.'

Sam Corbett
Managing Editor
Monash Mt Eliza Business Review

'The concept of a zoo as an analogy for customer service is appropriate. For many of us, understanding the needs and wants of our customers is as foreign as understanding the behaviour of the zoo animals. Cathy De Vrye's book opens the gate at the zoo for those of us who are dedicated to customer service but are unsure how to deliver it.'

Bruce Ingrey
Ray White Real Estate

'Cathy has a very easy, open and natural style of writing that makes this book extremely easy to read . . . it approaches the subject in a fashion that is easily comprehended.'

Kylee Gardiner
Training Consultant, Optus Communications

'Great ideas for small business—an easy-to-read book with comments which I could readily relate to.'

Kaeren Martin
Owner, Peeping Tom Curtains
PLUS Ingrey quote attached

'A thoroughly enjoyable story . . . The 'Zoo' would be a valuable component in any service improvement program.'

Wing Commander Mal Treglown,
RAAF

About the author

Catherine de Vrye is an outstanding communicator with proven international experience in the private and public sectors. She received the 1993 Australian Executive Woman of the Year Award and is the author of the best-selling *Good Service is Good Business*.

Catherine has spoken on 5 continents to Fortune 500 companies, small businesses and sporting and public sector organisations. Her delightfully humorous approach to presenting serious content has earned her repeat business among clients such as American Express, AT&T, Australian Tourism, Coca-Cola, Ernst & Young, 3M, Mercedes, Qantas, Red Cross, Royal Australian Airforce and the World Triathlon Championships.

Catherine was an executive with IBM for a decade, holding numerous roles in sales and marketing, communications and management development. She spent two years in Tokyo as Asia Pacific Headquarters Personnel Manager where she gained first-hand experience of service quality and regional uniqueness.

In the public sector, Catherine has been a board member of the NSW Police Force (the third largest in the world) and the CEO of Junior Achievement Australia. She has worked for Ministers of Consumer Affairs, Education and also Sport where she was involved in the establishment of the award-winning 'Life. Be In It' fitness campaign.

Catherine holds a Master of Science degree and has attended short courses at Harvard and the Monash Mt Eliza Business School where she is a frequent guest lecturer; but her belief is that the most important education is turning common sense into common practice!

THE CUSTOMER SERVICE ZOO

Catherine DeVrye

ALLEN & UNWIN

First published in 1999 by
Allen & Unwin
9 Atchison Street
St Leonards NSW 1590
Australia
Phone: (61 2) 8425 0100
Fax: (61 2) 9906 2218
E-mail: frontdesk@allen-unwin.com.au
Web: http://www.allen-unwin.com.au

National Library of Australia
Cataloguing-in-Publication entry:

DeVrye, Catherine.
  The customer service zoo.

  Bibliography.
  ISBN 1 86508 005 5.

  1. Customer relations. 2. Customer services. I. Title.

658.812

Set in 12.5/15.5pt Fairfield by DOCUPRO, Sydney
Printed and bound by Australian Print Group, Maryborough

10 9 8 7 6 5 4 3 2 1

Contents

Acknowledgements

Thanks to Mum, Dad and Granddad for taking me to the zoo, when at an early age I delighted at the antics of the animals and later grew to appreciate the precious resources of our environment.

Time is also precious, and I would very much like to thank the following people for taking time out of their busy schedules to review the book: Kris Cole, Ben Dalton, Kaylee Gardiner, Clair Ridding, and especially Les Galbraith, Vice President of American Express Travel, for his innovative approach. They are valuable clients and friends. Thanks to all my other clients and speaking bureaus, which have provided opportunities for me to address thousands of people around the world and to listen to what those audiences have said they wanted to learn.

I would also like to thank James Falk and Josh Dowse for their valuable editorial assistance. Thanks to Josh's ability to brainstorm and communicate with care, this is a more user-friendly book.

My thanks go to Peter Broelman, an outstanding illustrator, who has brought the animals to life, also to all those individuals and organisations around the world that continually contribute to our human awareness of that animal life.

A percentage of the author's royalties has been donated to the RSPCA (NSW) in acknowledgement of their assistance to animals in need.

Introduction

Remember your childhood visits to the zoo? I can still recall those Sunday afternoon trips, perched on Dad's shoulders to see over the bigger people—to look into a world of wonder, fascinated by animal behaviour, as I am fascinated by people today.

It would be naive to suggest that the playfulness of children, cubs or puppies can provide solutions to our increasingly complex business world. But how often do we feel our places of employment are little more than cages to our creative spirit? I often hear such comments as 'It's a zoo out there'.

We grow older, and apart from wrinkles and grey

hair nothing seems to change. Except a growing resentment, or acceptance, of our unnatural condition; no longer having fun, feeling shackled by the mortgage. With the organisational chart providing as much freedom to move as a lion cage, we feel disempowered and trapped. This is especially true when dealing with the wide array of issues we face in providing quality customer service.

Until recently, I hadn't been to the zoo in years. I never seemed to have enough time. Life seemed simpler as a child, and Dad always seemed to have ready answers to my never-ending array of questions. As author of the best-selling *Good Service is Good Business* I have had the privilege of delivering presentations on five continents to leading business and government organisations. But lately the questions I get asked, and find myself asking, have changed dramatically. Now they're more likely to be:

☆ How to boost the bottom line?

☆ How to handle change?

☆ How to get more from employees?

☆ How to get more reliable suppliers?

☆ How to find more time and balance in our busy lives?

☆ How to have more loyal customers and more profitability?

☆ How to plan for the future?

As an executive in both the private and public sector for more than two decades, in two hemispheres, I have frequently wondered why we so often take pride in providing complex answers to such questions rather than relying on simplicity. In hindsight, many of the big corporate issues I faced at IBM, or in government, were handled easily once a simple solution had emerged from continuing intellectual analysis.

During my time as an executive in Japan, I learned about the Eastern calendar. For centuries it has been based on a 12-year cycle, symbolic of certain character traits. Similar to Zodiac star signs, birth in the Year of the Tiger or Year of the Rabbit is meant to lend you certain character attributes. As animal analogies have always been used it didn't seem too crazy to use them in a book on customer service.

This is not a text, and it contains no earth-shattering revelations. Rather, it is a simple story, which you can quickly and easily digest, especially written for those of you who are trying to provide better customer service in your organisation and who sometimes feel that you're the only ones who care!

So, for the next little while, suspend your sophisticated, adult beliefs about what business books should be, and enjoy your visit to the zoo.

Friday night

It hadn't been a good week. In fact, the past month had been nothing but one headache after another at the office—more customer complaints, less profit, and a seemingly endless array of staff morale issues.

Phil wasn't in the best frame of mind when he arrived home on Friday night. He loosened his tie with one hand, turning the company car into the driveway with the other. He was looking forward to a cold drink and watching some football on TV. As he grabbed his briefcase from the back seat, he remembered he had to work on the customer service strategy over the weekend. It wasn't an appealing thought. At least it could wait until after golf on Saturday.

Their fat Labrador was the only one to greet him as he tripped over a suitcase by the front door. 'What's this doing here?' he snapped.

'I'll be right down, dear', called his wife Karen, as she came down the stairs. She was obviously distressed. 'I've got to visit Mum. The nursing home called to say that she'd taken a turn for the worse—so you'll have to look after the kids for the weekend. I've arranged for Steve to stay with a school friend, but you'll have to have Julie.'

This was the last thing Phil needed after a bad week at work. But what could he say? So much for a relaxing game of golf, he thought.

'Couldn't you take Julie with you?' he asked.

'To a nursing home?' Karen exclaimed. She gave him 'the look', and his resistance was overcome by guilt. 'Heat up dinner in the microwave, and she can watch videos until 8 pm. I'll see you Sunday.'

'Yeah, OK. I, uh, hope your mother feels a bit better.' She was already gone without even a good-bye kiss.

Phil managed the microwave with minimum fuss, and then delved into a tub of ice-cream in the freezer. 'This cooking isn't all that difficult', he thought, forgetting that it had all been prepared for him. After dinner he settled down with a drink in front of the television in the study. Julie seemed content to watch the TV in the family room. 'This weekend might not be so bad after all', he thought. He soon dozed off watching the football.

He woke to Julie shaking him, almost pulling his arm out of its socket. 'Wake up, Dad. Wake up', she was whining. 'I'm tired. It's time for bed. You want to read me a story?'

It was more than an hour past her bedtime when he tucked her in.

'What are we gonna do tomorrow, Dad? Can we go to the zoo?'

'We'll see', said Phil. 'If you promise to be very quiet in the morning . . . maybe.'

'Please Dad, please', she pleaded.

'We'll see!' The last thing he needed was another demand on his time. Surely time had become the principal luxury of life, displacing champagne and caviar!

'Now, be a good girl and go to sleep. Night, night, Princess', he whispered, kissing her on the forehead.

'She's really a good kid, but I can't think of anything worse than going to the zoo. It's been a zoo at work all week', was his last thought as his head hit the pillow.

Saturday morning

Morning came too quickly. When Phil stumbled down to the kitchen he found Julie, the Labrador, and half a box of cereal spread out over the floor. Julie was watching cartoons; the dog had his gaze more firmly fixed on the cereal.

'Can we go to the zoo now, Dad? You promised.'

Kids. They only remembered what they wanted to. Just like most of his employees. 'I did not promise. I said we'd see! And besides, it's not open yet. Now I've got some work to do this morning, so if you watch TV for a while we'll talk about it later.'

4

Phil opened his briefcase and thought about the customer service strategy. Why bother? Sometimes he thought he was the only one who cared. His boss always seemed preoccupied with financial details. The rest of senior management agreed it was a problem—but someone else's! And some of the employees just wanted to go through the motions and get home as soon as possible. 'We're only successful because most of our employees and managers do it right on their own, not because our system helps them', he thought.

Phil sensed that something had to be done to get and keep happy customers—but didn't know what that 'something' could possibly be. Candon International was doing OK—it was a successful multinational—but he knew it could be much better. Across the board, from financial and insurance services to manufacturing and pharmaceuticals, all employees could improve in how they treated customers. And it wasn't just frontline clerks: it covered everyone from tradesmen to underwriters and managers.

Phil knew what to aim for: not just satisfied customers but delighted ones, customers who'd personally recommend the business to others. He knew it was important—he always remembered that it cost five times more to get a new customer than to keep an existing one. 'How can I make us different from our competition? How can I make our customers, staff, suppliers and shareholders understand how important superior service is?'

Phil asked himself. The task seemed daunting for the entire management team, let alone for his customer service strategy.

Where to start? Management had prepared strategic plans before, and everyone had had their say. But these plans hardly ever turned into concrete action. Management talked about the ideas, they were tabled at board meetings, and a program with some clever slogan was put in place for a few months and then forgotten. The only thing the plans ever did was collect dust. Improving service was the first thing talked about and the last thing actually done.

Phil wondered if he was wasting his Saturday morning. All he'd done so far was chew the top of his pencil. But the CEO had specifically asked him to come up with a customer service strategy to improve profitability. He knuckled down to getting something on paper.

After two hours, Phil had typed seven pages into his laptop PC. It had everything: the standard executive summary, table of contents, statistics, recommended management initiatives, proposed staff actions, suggested promotional and incentive campaigns, customer satisfaction measurements and, of course, recommendations to hire a consultant. Phil was happy to have something on paper, but he was worried that it was a lot like the last plan. And what would happen to it? After all, strategic plans are useless unless turned into strategic action.

'I've got something to show the CEO, but it's not going to do the job', Phil thought. 'I've got no idea of how to do something different—something that will work. And if I don't come up with something, it's more than my reputation on the line.' He closed his laptop with a sigh.

That was the signal Julie had been waiting for. 'Is the zoo open now, Dad? Can we go? Can we?'

'OK, OK. Have you brushed your teeth? Got your hat?'

Service is a journey

They arrived at the zoo at precisely the same time as every other household within a 20-kilometre radius—or so it seemed. The parking lot was like dodge 'ems at the amusement park: there weren't any signs and cars were going in all directions. After jostling for a parking space for 15 minutes, Phil finally squeezed in, only a mini-marathon from the entrance. He *was* exaggerating, but who's logical on a stinking hot Saturday afternoon?

A queue of people were waiting to pay. 'You're kidding. There are four turnstiles, and only two are open. What's wrong with this place?'

The ticket-seller overheard him. 'I'm sorry sir, but one of our staff is sick and someone else is at lunch. Here's your ticket. Have a nice day.'

'Yeah, right.' Phil caught himself being rude in front of Julie. He kept his next thoughts to himself. 'This isn't my idea of a good time. What a hassle! Parking's lousy, there aren't enough staff, and those they have are fake-friendly. No-one's made it easy for me to do business with the zoo. If the rest is like this I won't be coming back.' This sort of thing wouldn't happen at his business . . . or would it? Phil winced at the thought. Unfortunately, he knew the answer. 'It's only by accident that our service is any good', he thought.

Only Julie's excitement seemed undiminished by this bad start to the day.

'C'mon Dad. Let's go see the monkeys first. They're my favourite.'

'You're my favourite little monkey', Phil teased, as he ruffled her hair. Julie made it easier to relax a little.

The ape enclosure was a short stroll away. For the first time that day Phil found himself interested in something. He even started to forget the lousy service. 'They're so big, and so human', he thought. 'These ape characters are just like an office crowd. They sit around in small clusters, content to quietly chat with each other and munch away on the monkey equivalent of coffee and biscuits.'

Meanwhile, a larger male gained the attention of the crowd by heartily thumping his chest in a display of dominance. His shiny chest looked almost unreal, just like King Kong. Phil smiled at the thought of his previous boss—just like the gorilla, he always wanted to be the centre of attention and went out of his way to sing his own praises to anyone who would listen. No matter what Phil or his colleagues achieved, this guy always stole the limelight, took personal credit for their achievements, and was quick to point the finger at others for any mistakes. Phil made a mental note to publicly congratulate Jane in accounts. The suggestion she made a few weeks ago could save the company thousands of dollars. 'Me Tarzan, you Jane', he said to Julie.

She ignored him. 'Look, Dad. This monkey with the black tail likes me. If I clap, it claps. Watch.' Julie's enthusiasm brought Phil's mind back to the situation at hand. Sure enough, if she clapped once, the animal would do likewise. If she clapped twice, it repeated her actions precisely.

'Monkey see, monkey do, darling', he said. Come to think of it, things weren't much different in the office, he thought; his employees invariably copied what management did. It didn't matter whether the managers were a positive or negative influence. What people saw them do was twice as powerful as what they said. When it comes to leadership, actions always speak louder than words.

For the first time that day, Phil had an original idea about his customer service strategy. He realised it was no use coming out with trite phrases like 'the customer comes first' if employees saw managers ignore a ringing telephone or avoid returning customer messages. It was pointless trying to enforce dress standards on the front line if a manager never cared enough to have the soup stains removed from his designer tie. Or talking about service if managers parked in the customer-only spots when they were in a hurry, or posted staff notices with spelling errors and incorrect grammar.

> **When it comes to leadership, actions always speak louder than words.**

Phil couldn't help but think of the founders of IBM and McDonald's. Tom Watson and Ray Croc would be horrified if they realised that those managers who followed them didn't always follow their leadership example of always picking up a piece of paper in the parking lot, even though they were the CEO—thus sending a signal to everyone in the organisation that cleanliness and attention to detail were important.

'I love how we managers talk about customer service when we haven't been near an actual customer in years', he thought. 'Hypocritical. But making a top team spend one day a week face-to-face with customers probably doesn't put it right either.' It might be OK in small organisations, but in bigger ones they'd be the highest paid and least efficient counter staff in existence. It could even affect how well they managed. But putting managers on the front line maybe once or twice a year could give them some practical service ideas. It would also signal to every employee that management thought serving customers was important. And it would emphasise that those customers paid the salary of every employee, even those with no direct customer contact.

It was clear that 'Monkey see, monkey do' was not restricted to the confines of cages at the zoo. It was imperative that management lead by example. To get great service, management had to understand that if you weren't serving a customer, you should be serving someone who was.[1]

One of the apes let out a series of ear-splitting hoots and screeches that dragged Phil back to where he was. He was annoyed at himself for getting caught up with work again. 'Oh well, that's one more idea than I thought I'd get today', Phil said to himself. 'Not that it'll save me on Monday.'

Julie tugged impatiently at his jacket. 'I want to see the lions, Dad.'

As they started to leave the apes, Phil noticed a bronze plaque showing the species, genus, family

12

and order of each animal. 'Order, mmmh.' He liked the idea of order. And he was conscious that the lions were at the opposite end of the zoo. 'Sweetheart, we've just seen the apes. What letter of the alphabet does the word ape begin with?'

Julie replied 'A, Dad, silly . . . Why?'

'Well', said Phil, 'now let's go to your favourite animal whose name starts with a B . . .'

Bear

'B is for bears, Dad! We'll see the bears next. And then C for camels. And then D for dingoes, and then . . .'

As Julie reeled off the animals, Phil wondered if he'd created a monster of his own. With a bit of luck she'd be worn out before he was forced to visit the entire animal alphabet. Then he'd be able to get back to work on that $%&$^@#$* customer service strategy.

But, on second thoughts, he'd got a good idea out of the apes. Maybe he could pick up a few more where he was. And look after Julie at the same time. 'Yeah', he thought. 'That's what we need. A simple approach that everyone can identify with. An ABC of customer service, using animal analogies.' It would certainly be a strategy unlike any of the others tucked away in bottom drawers.

Phil's thoughts were now racing faster than Julie's little feet, as she headed in the direction of the bears. He now felt he had a direction of his own worth pursuing. Already he had a tentative title for his presentation on Monday morning: 'Customer service . . . it's a zoo out there. But it doesn't need to be!' He might at least get his colleagues' attention for a few seconds—until they dismissed him as crazy. 'All I've got to do is brainstorm a few ideas while I walk around', he thought.

> **Customer service . . . it's a zoo out there. But it doesn't need to be!**

But staring at the huge black bear, Phil couldn't see any connection to service at all. All he could think of was a recent customer satisfaction survey, which had indicated more dissatisfaction than the previous one. Phil couldn't understand why. Customers were more demanding and less willing to accept mediocre service quality. In fact, 67% of consumers[2] had higher expectations than five years ago. And the more competitive the marketplace, the more important it was to exceed those expectations and delight customers.

Meanwhile, most of Candon's managers were

happily hibernating in their corner office caves, oblivious to what was happening outside, Phil thought. They'd analyse the survey data, growl at some employees, blame the economy and request another report. It never occurred to them to venture into the wilds and speak to real customers themselves. After all, that was someone else's job—they were executives.

Phil laughed out loud at the analogy, which seemed to be getting cornier by the second. But it made sense. Maybe the bear was relevant to service after all. It was time for the top team to come out of hibernation. He decided to recommend that each manager call at least one existing customer a day and one former customer a week. It wouldn't take much time, and he was sure that they'd gather useful information, just as the bear gathered juicy berries in the wild. It wouldn't be sanitised and filtered by others; so managers would get to hear the real story, not what subordinates wanted them to hear or thought they wanted to hear.

Phil searched for some way to sum up the point. 'We've got to come out of hibernation or the market will be bearish on our stocks.' That should get the director's attention. 'And, after all, if we don't have service quality we don't have customers and we don't have jobs.' That should get the interest of his colleagues.

Camel

Phil was still thinking about how he could convince his peers to step outside their comfort zone when he and Julie reached the camel enclosure. 'A horse designed by a committee', he thought. He'd been on enough committees to appreciate that old joke.

Julie ran up to the fence, leaving Phil with his musings. The 'ship of the desert', spitting, Bedouin caravans, camel races, two humps or three . . . he watched Julie squeal as a camel came closer. 'It's a tough life in the desert; you have to fight for everything', he thought. 'When it comes down to the basics, camels compete for scarce resources in a harsh climate. Just as in business. And they've got an advantage: they're legendary for storing water to avoid dehydration. No constant trips to the coffee machine for them!'

Phil read the plaque on the fence, and was surprised to see that camels evolved in North America but died out there after spreading around the world. He imagined camels pulling the wagons westward, or a camelless carriage instead of a horseless one. He laughed at the picture.

Phil's brainstorming was getting bogged down. What had this got to do with service? Phil gave up for a while and thought about his committee colleagues. 'We spend most of our time squabbling over who gets what, and forget that the real competition is external. Sometimes it seems we care more about looking good than doing good. And half of them think that we'll boost our bottom line just by freezing expenses.'

> **The real competition is external.**

Phil got angry just thinking about their narrow-mindedness. 'It won't make a difference unless we focus on competition outside the company—unless we make the best of what we've got to meet it', he thought. 'In a tough environment we need all our resources working together to meet external challenges. Just as the camel stores up reserves of water for the challenge of the desert, so we need to collect all our resources for what's important. And we need to give up on protecting our own patches in committee meetings.'

Phil thought about what resources these might be: new thoughts that staff contributed to improve the business; ways of improving processes, quality and costs; ways of adding value. 'It may cost a little in the beginning, but we have to do it to compete', he thought.

Phil was happy with his idea; he strode off to the dingoes, Julie bouncing alongside. He was starting to believe that his brainstorming was going to work, and he knew just where it was going.

As usually happens when you think you know where you're headed, he was in for a surprise.

Dingo

'These dingoes look pretty harmless', Phil thought. They didn't seem at all predatory, as the sign suggested. But then, not every danger was obvious. Even little lapdogs could take your finger off. And there were plenty of lapdogs at the office. Friendly to the ones that fed them, but dangerous to all the rest. Especially Harry in accounts: butter wouldn't melt in his mouth, but he never had a good word to say about anyone.

'Why are some people always so negative?' Phil wondered. 'Even customers always focus on what goes wrong rather than what goes right. I'm sure

I've read somewhere that customers are more than twice as likely to remember their negative experiences with an organisation than their positive ones—if they bother to remember their experiences at all.[3] Maybe it is just human nature to pick on the bad stuff—which probably explains why we don't see any "Look out: nice dog" signs.'

Phil had owned a lot of dogs in his time—he liked them. His family had always liked them. They'd even shown dogs for a while, until his grandfather had got too old. Even now he could hear a saying his grandfather often quoted to him when he was a boy: 'A dog is man's best friend because it wags its tail instead of its tongue.'

Phil suddenly felt guilty. 'This brainstorming has turned around and bitten me', he thought. 'I'm part of the problem. That's not what I wanted to find out.'

> **Customers are more than twice as likely to remember their negative experiences with an organisation than their positive ones.**

He had put the boot into Harry, but when was the last time he'd said something complimentary about his staff, or another department? He'd certainly told Margaret in data-processing what he thought of her team last week. And it wasn't good. He made a mental note to find something positive to say to someone at work each and every day. In fact, he'd put it on his 'To do' list for the first few weeks, until it became a habit.

'Yeah, but I don't want to sound like that guy at the zoo ticket office, just mouthing the words', he thought. He was determined that his staff should trust him to be positive, rather than expect him to speak to them only when they had done something wrong. 'But will this do anything except make people feel better?' he asked himself. 'Is it worth my time to be positive?'

One of the zoo staff gave Julie a bone for the dingoes. She threw it to the dingo pup close to her, the one chasing its tail. Phil laughed, the bone reminding him of a joke someone had told at the golf club last week.

A blind man and his dog weave in and out of the traffic across a major street. After they miraculously reach the other side in one piece, the blind man reaches in his pocket to give the dog a biscuit. A passer-by, witnessing the dangerous crossing, says: 'If I were you I wouldn't reward that incompetent dog—it almost got you killed.'

The blind man responds: 'I'm not rewarding it, I'm just finding its mouth so I can kick it in the butt!'

'A lot of staff would relate to that joke', thought Phil; 'but Candon does pretty well, the quality division especially.' Their manager was always telling her staff how well they were doing. But Phil recalled visiting a few client companies where all

22

he heard was managers giving staff a boot in the butt, just like the dog.

His grandfather often said that you could judge someone's quality by how they treated their pets. 'People aren't dogs', thought Phil. 'But there are some things management could learn from them about creating loyalty and trust in humans. It's the same for both: clear expectations, rewards for desired behaviour and, if necessary, punishment for continually getting it wrong. But how often do we treat people that way?'

'What do I get for being positive with staff?' he asked himself again. 'They'll trust me, at least. And they'll be able to take some initiative without fear of my coming down hard on them. And be honest with me about what's going on.' This dog idea was giving him some good material. But what was the story that trainer had told at his induction seminar 15 years ago? Something about training guide dogs for the blind? He was sure it was useful.

His memory slowly started to clear: 'There are two sorts of dogs that flunk out of guide dog school', she began. 'One is the dog that is totally disobedient. It tears up your possessions, growls, and refuses to stay calmly on the lead. You'd expect that sort of dog to fail. But, strange as it sounds, the other sort of dog that fails is the one that is totally obedient.'

Phil's puzzlement had disappeared when she explained: 'Imagine you're blind and at a major intersection. You tell your dog "Go!" Without

questioning, without checking, without thinking
. . . it goes. Whether a semi-trailer is coming or
not.'

The trainer went on: 'The dogs that passed were
the ones labelled "selectively disobedient"—with
emphasis on the word "selectively". They assess
the safety of the situation and then obey only if
it is safe. They disobey if obeying would harm you.
In modern organisations, ideal employees also
need to be selectively disobedient. They don't obey
without thinking of the consequences. They don't
assume that the boss is
always right and has all the
answers just because he or
she is the boss.'

> **Ideal employees need
> to be selectively
> disobedient.**

Phil searched his memory
for the key to creating this
autonomy, this selective dis-
obedience. He couldn't remember what she had
said, so he had to think it through for himself.
Maybe it was like training dogs; maybe it was
about creating a relationship of trust in the
organisation, just as you do with an animal. Maybe
it was about being positive, supporting people and
the decisions they make for the good of the company. That way no-one, no matter how low they
might be on the pecking order, would be fright-
ened to turn to the boss and say: 'Hey, I think
there's a better way.'

Phil could see that this sort of corporate culture
would let staff give people the service they needed,

even if the rules had to be bent. And it would save management from being stuck in 'the rules' until the semitrailer equivalent of the competition flattened the organisation. The dingoes had shown Phil more than he could have imagined: it was important to focus on creating an environment that instilled long-term loyalty and trust, because that way staff would treat customers the way they wanted to be treated. If you didn't look after your staff, they wouldn't look after your customers.

Of course, when he was explaining this he'd have to emphasise that the message was not that they should treat employees like dogs, as one or two of the office cynics might suggest. Still, Phil was optimistic that . . . he just might be able to teach old dogs new tricks after all!

Elephant

The sign on the next enclosure read:

Weighing 5–6 tons, the African elephant is the largest and most powerful of all living land mammals. It is also one of the most gentle and social of all animals, a vegetarian living in peaceful family units.

Phil watched as an elephant calf followed her mother, holding onto her tail with its trunk. The calf bleated in a surprisingly squeaky way. Julie giggled and pulled him to the fence, her hand small in his.

'It's possible to be strong *and* gentle', Phil thought. 'To have control but give people the chance to take charge of what they do. That's what empowerment is.' He finally understood all the books he'd read—books like Belasco's *Teaching the Elephant to Dance*.[4] Elephants have so much power they could use to make a change, but so few of them do. 'Belasco's book will be a great way to introduce the idea of empowerment', he thought. 'It fits with my animals, the story's great and says it better than I ever could. But how does the story go?' he asked himself.

Phil sat watching the elephants with Julie on his lap. Bit by bit, parts of the book came back. Since time immemorial, handlers chain young elephants to stakes driven deep into the ground. The calves can't pull out the stakes, so they learn that they can't leave. As they grow older and stronger, the elephants still do not try to leave, even though as adults they have the strength to pull out the stake. Their handlers eventually replace the chains with a small metal bracelet which reinforces the conditioning: the adult elephant thinks it still can't escape.

Belasco suggests that large companies are no different from elephants: they remain constrained by earlier ways of doing things, by procedures and rules, and believe there is no alternative. But if the circus tent catches on fire and the elephant smells the smoke, it forgets its conditioning and runs away. The emergency overrides what's been learnt. Management's task is to create a sense of urgency for change, so that employees see the 'flames' and smell the 'smoke' without actually needing to see the tent burned to the ground!

'This is great', Phil thought. 'There's no better way to explain empowerment. It's about breaking down barriers and knowing you can act. But what can management do to develop this? And how can this urgency be focused in the right direction?'

Phil stared at the elephants, hoping that his brainstorming success would continue. It did, as he remembered an old Sufi tale.

As three blind men encounter an elephant, each exclaims aloud.

'It is a large, tough thing, wide and broad like a rug', says the first, grasping an ear.

The second, holding the trunk, says: 'I have the real facts. It is a straight and hollow pipe.'

The third, holding the front leg, says: 'It is mighty and firm like a pillar.'

They didn't appreciate that the whole was greater than the sum of the parts. Are the three blind men any different from the heads of manufacturing, marketing and research in many companies? Each can clearly see the problems of the organisation from their own perspective but none see how the policies of their department interact with the others. Interestingly, the Sufi story concludes by observing that given these men's ways of knowing, they will never know an elephant.

Phil knew his company would never be able to answer customer needs until all employees and managers realised they could pull free from imaginary constraints, and until they used their combined strength to contribute to a shared, bigger picture.

More elephants had joined the calf and cow; now a chain of four elephants gracefully swayed in unison in front of him, each holding the tail of the one in front.

> **Management's task is to create a sense of urgency for change.**

Moving together came naturally to them. It was like one long tail relay; in fact, a relay was a good way to think about business. Every individual had to add value with each step—add value for each process along the customer chain. All had to work together to ensure smooth links from one process to another and from one department to another. Any team was only as strong as the weakest link.

Come to think of it, the food chain itself was an excellent example. His uncle, who ran a dairy farm, once told Phil that it took over a kilogram of grain from the wheat farmer down the road for a cow to produce a litre of milk. Then there was the pasteurisation process, the packaging, the printing, the wholesale and retail outlets and, of course, the myriad distribution channels along the way; all necessary steps which the average consumer took for granted as they poured milk on their morning cereal. And of course, going right back before the cow even ate the grain, there were the agronomists, fertilizer producers, suppliers of irrigation pipe, crop sprayers, manufacturers of tractors and their various components. The list of the links seemed endless.

As he walked away, Phil could see how empowerment was embodied in elephants. Elephants revealed the urgent need to let people break free and act on their own; the need for overall vision to guide that urgency; the need for teamwork to get things done. With those ideas, Candon would be able to give the service Phil was looking for. 'I might just be getting something I can use', he said.

'What did you say, Daddy?' asked Julie.

He dragged her off in search of the next letter.

Fish

Julie stuck her mouth against the aquarium glass, puffing out her cheeks and fogging it up. Phil thought she looked like the guppy swimming towards her.

'Fish stories: there are a lot of them', he thought. 'The one that got away, big fish, little fish, Jonah, Moby Dick . . .' He tried hard to find something he could use. His eyes settled on a trout on the bottom of the aquarium in front of him. The last fish he had caught was a trout. 'I haven't been fishing in a long time', he thought. 'It's time I taught the kids to fish.'

'Give a man a fish and he eats for a day, teach a man to fish and he eats for a lifetime.' It was an oldie, but it could be a starting point; it was about giving people the skills they needed to do the job. Maybe it could relate to letting employees think for themselves, rather than handing them rules. After all, empowerment was about teaching employees how to 'fish', rather than making them feel lost if the boss wasn't around to give instructions.

> Give a man a fish and he eats for a day; teach a man to fish and he eats for a lifetime.

Phil thought it through. You taught staff to fish by giving them basic product and technical training. You supplied the basic tools, and gave constructive tips if the big one got away. You encouraged them by creating a trusting and respectful work environment—and that produced self-esteem and team morale. You encouraged them to take ownership of their own fishing hole and equipment and to feel responsible for the end result. And then you let them fish!

'What happens if we do that?' Phil asked himself. 'They'll make decisions on the spot that relate directly to the customer. After all, they're in the best position to do it. Once they're ready, they're the ones who'll know best. Like that young guy at the supermarket', he thought.

A supermarket manager friend told Phil about a supermarket that held regular breakfast meetings with customers, to find out exactly what their perceptions of the store were. One woman mentioned that the fish was quite good, but that it would be better if it were fresh. Staff seemed surprised by her comment, as it *was* fresh. They asked her to explain. She argued that it couldn't possibly be fresh, because it was packed in plastic wrap.

Now, the store didn't try to convince her that her perception was wrong, because they knew that you seldom win an argument without losing a customer. They initially dismissed her comment. But a young employee had listened to all this, and finally spoke up. He suggested that they do a little experiment when the fish arrived the next morning. The manager agreed, so they packaged half as before, while they laid out the other half on freshly crushed ice. Much to their amazement, they sold nearly twice as much of the fish on ice. What's more, they made more profit because packaging and labour costs were lower.

All this was truly amazing, considering that the customer had been wrong! In reality the fish was fresh, but her perception, and the perceptions of others, were that wrapped fish must be frozen.

Of course, Phil knew that the perceptions people have are real for them, and whether those perceptions are right or wrong it is almost impossible to argue with them. But the supermarket management would never have found that out if they had not listened to the young employee, and let him test out his ideas. Maybe it was not only customers whose perceptions could be wrong: how many managers thought staff couldn't make decisions without them?

'Give them the tools and they'll do better than we can', Phil thought.

Giraffe

'What is the animal with a long neck?' asked Phil. He stretched his head up as high as he could. Julie laughed and shouted 'Giraffe!'

When they got there, Phil looked up more than six metres to the top of the tallest animal. The giraffe reached skyward to pluck a leaf from a branch. Phil stretched his neck again and felt a vertebra click. 'What neck pain those things must have', he thought. 'Too much time at the PC for me. I've got to get some more exercise. Maybe yoga could fix this neck.'

'How far can giraffes see from up there, Daddy?' asked Julie.

'A really long way, Princess', Phil said. 'When they look around them they can see every part of where they live, and they always know if a lion is coming to get them.'

'And how high do they reach to eat things?'

'As high as they have to', he answered. 'When the zookeeper puts it at the bottom, they don't reach very far. When he puts it at the top, they stretch right up until they get it.'

'What a perspective that would be', thought Phil. Aim high, achieve high. That's what Stormin' Norman Schwartzkopf had done.

Early on in his army days, Schwartzkopf was given responsibility for army helicopter maintenance. When he asked how many helicopters were available to fly on any given day, the response was always the same: '75%, Sir.'

Aim high to achieve high.

After a while, he asked why availability was always precisely 75%. He received the reply: 'That's the minimum standard, Sir.'

Stormin' Norman replied: 'Well, as of today, the minimum standard is 85%.' And, sure enough, within a short time 85% of helicopters were ready to fly.

Phil realised that too often his own firm settled for the standards of the past, rather than aiming for higher levels of customer satisfaction. It had worked in the past, because they'd made good profits and kept growing.

'We've got to set our sights high but still keep our feet firmly on the ground', muttered Phil. He vowed to increase the minimum customer satisfaction ratings over the next year, and to focus on continual improvement, just as his local pizza shop had gradually reduced its delivery time guarantee from 45 minutes to 20. He knew he might be sticking his neck out a bit with his colleagues, but if they continued to do what they had always done they would inevitably get what they had always got. And that simply wasn't good enough in Phil's book.

'Whew . . . if I'm going to remember all this, I'd better start writing it down', he thought. He searched throught his pockets—and came up with some crumpled business cards. 'These will have to do', he thought. 'If the ideas aren't simple enough to fit on here, I'm not using them.'

Horse

By this time Julie was tired of watching animals, and wanted a little more activity. 'Can I have a pony ride, Dad? Please?'

'OK, cowgirl.'

Phil bought a ticket. He'd gladly have paid twice the price for the look of delight on his daughter's face. She sat beaming atop a white spotted pony. 'I wish all my customers were as happy as yours', he said casually to the stablehand in charge.

'It's pretty easy for me', the hand replied, 'All I gotta do is give 'em what they want. That puts a smile on their faces.'

'Is that all there is to it?' asked Phil.

'It's got to be safe and clean, but all we really have to do is match a kid to a pony.'

Only then did Phil notice the variety of ponies tied to the fence. Julie sat on a small, placid-looking one, much to his relief.

'Yep, it's horses for courses!' laughed the stable-hand.

Phil shook his head. It was so obvious. It was just common sense; give people what they want, treat them as individuals. All customer service was pretty simple. But the corporate challenge was to turn common sense into common practice. And best practice into common practice. 'Yeah, it's true', thought Phil. 'Everyone's different and needs to be treated that way.' Yet how often were they reduced to the lowest common denominator and treated the same?

As Julie rode around, Phil leaned on the wooden railing and thought of watching John Wayne movies with his grandfather. That was a while ago, but he still remembered Grandpa laughing at his own joke about John Wayne and the movie 'True Grit':

These two guys went to see 'True Grit'. John Wayne fell off his horse in that movie. Well, John Wayne never falls off his horse. One of the men had seen it before, so he bet his buddy five bucks that John Wayne would fall off his horse. Naturally his friend took the bet, thinking that John Wayne never fell off his horse. As they came out of the picture theatre he reached into his pocket to pay the bet, muttering that he couldn't believe John Wayne had fallen off his horse. His friend refused to accept it, admitting that he'd seen the movie before and had tricked his friend into the bet.

The other replied: 'Well, I'd seen it before too, but I didn't reckon he'd fall off twice!'

Grandpa always used to say that some people just didn't have horse sense. Horse sense, common sense, whatever it was, companies certainly needed it. Grandpa also used to say: 'Phil, mistakes are inevitable. But learning from mistakes is optional.' Those two guys at the movie didn't learn!

> Customer service doesn't have to use grand theory and big ideas—common sense is enough.

'It's only common sense to learn from where we've gone wrong', thought Phil. 'If we haven't treated customers as special individuals in the past, then we'll do it from now on. Customer service doesn't have to use grand theory and big ideas—common sense is enough. And it's only common sense to be customer-driven. There's a quote from some Ford executive about it . . . *If we're not customer-driven, our cars won't be either!*' said Phil out loud.

'Are you all right?' asked the stablehand. He

looked at Phil oddly. Phil took Julie's hand as she dismounted and mumbled that he was fine as he walked away.

'This brainstorming thing is working, but it's starting to get embarrassing', he thought.

Impala

As Julie raced over to the impala enclosure, Phil sat down and let the redness slowly disappear from his cheeks. 'The car industry's gone through a lot of change; maybe there's something I can use there besides a quote from Ford', he thought. All he could come up with was another quote from cowboy philosopher, Will Rogers: *Even if you're on the right track, you'll get run over if you just stand there.* 'What does that mean?' Phil asked himself.

He gave up and looked at the animals. As he gazed at the impalas grazing placidly, he remembered seeing them jump and run on a National

Geographic TV special. Those graceful, deer-like animals take off at the slightest noise or movement. They're attuned to even the minutest changes in their environment. They're constantly alert to the scent of a predator on the wind. Just as organisations need to be alert to the winds of change. Impalas can never assume that any territory is so safe they can do as they please.

And the impala need to be able to change direction quickly, because their lives depend on it. It's the only way they can shake off what threatens them. So, too, does everyone in an organisation have to be aware of the need to change direction when necessary and to do it quickly. Paralysis by analysis doesn't only kill impalas: it has wiped out many an immobile organisation. And individuals weren't immune either. How many times had Phil heard people talk about their ideas but never follow through on them: 'I'm gonna do this. I'm gonna do that' turns into 'I could have done that'. Yet they can die without ever getting around to taking any action. Phil could see that often companies didn't move as quickly as they should when confronted by a predatory competitor—and certainly not like an impala fighting for its life on the open veldt.

'We're more likely to react as if we're dazed by

> **An organisation has to be aware of the need to change direction when necessary and to do it quickly.**

the headlights of an oncoming car', thought Phil. 'If we do that, we'll get run over by the competition. We've got to monitor what's going on and move forward to evade it, or overcome it.' He scribbled a few ideas on the cards. Giraffe: stretch higher; impala: move fast; elephant: urgency for empowerment. What was the horse? he worried. Common sense!

Phil leant back with his hands clasped behind his head. He could relax. The observations for the strategy were coming fast and he was hardly even trying.

Joey

Moving along to the kangaroos, Phil was on a high. It was as if he'd had more coffee than he could handle. As the roos came into view, he recalled a trip to the outback and how he had been so worried about hitting one.

As he and Julie came closer, a joey hopped away and dived headfirst into its mother's pouch. It was hard to imagine that the cute little thing peeking out of the pouch would soon stand taller than a human. Phil was surprised to read that an adult male could disembowel a person with one powerful kick of its hind legs. 'Each seemingly sweet and innocuous thing holds some danger', he thought. 'How often has one small mistake kicked the guts out of a customer relationship?'

He knew his company normally met customer expectations; but he also knew that doing just one thing blatantly wrong could be fatal to the relationship. The other day a worker at a bank had told him he was the only complainant out of 12,074 people who had received a form letter from the bank. 'Boy, that really annoyed me', thought Phil.

> People don't want to be treated as a number or statistic, but as individuals.

'But, just like horses for courses, people don't want to be treated as a number or as a statistic! I don't mind a word-processed letter and I don't care whether 12,073 or 12,075 were happy; I want to be treated like an individual.' How much better it would be if they approached every request with the attitude that if the customer said 'Jump', the organisation would ask 'How high?' 'After all, we're not in the service business. We're in the people business', thought Phil. 'What counts is not what we give people, but the people we give it to. If they're not happy, everything else makes no difference. And come to think of it, I feel better myself if I can put a smile on someone's face.'

Phil chuckled, remembering a colleague who never seemed satisfied with the menu and always wanted to make modifications, even to his cup of coffee. He'd ask for a decaffeinated, skim-milk cappuccino with extra froth, and faithfully returned to the same café which cheerfully gave him a little jug of milk on the side so he could mix it to his exact specifications. Phil was sure the waitress thought his colleague was weird but never gave an inkling of her thoughts; now half of his department went there for coffee.

If an organisation wanted to reap the benefits of repeat business, they would be well advised to remember the WOMBAT principle (named after an Australian animal): in this you had one of the most powerful marketing tools on the planet— Word Of Mouth Best Advertising Technique. The only way to get a WOMBAT response was to jump higher than any customer ever expected.

'If we can remember that, we'll be leaps and bounds ahead of our competition', thought Phil. He congratulated himself on his attempt at humour as Julie pulled him in the direction of the next display. It was as though the kookaburra was laughing at his pun.

Kookaburra

Phil knew his company would be laughing all the way to the bank if they could reach a mass market and still give the impression of delivering per-sonalised service. But before he could brainstorm the idea, he had a more pressing problem to solve.

By now Julie was hungry and Phil was also feeling like a bite to eat, even though he had plenty of food for thought. A kiosk with tables was next to the koala enclosure, so they skipped past the kookaburra to sit down and refuel. As the koalas gobbled their gumleaves, Julie and Phil munched on hotdogs and chips. Phil was impressed by how clean the place was, and said so when a waiter cleared their table.

'Thank you sir. It's great to get the feedback; not many people bother. I seldom get to hear what people say because I'm the payroll manager. I don't meet customers that much', he said.

'You're the payroll manager and you're cleaning tables?' queried Phil.

'This is the one day each quarter when I work outside the office. Disney does it too. The director reckons it's a good way to remember why we have a job—because we have visitors like you and your little girl.'

> Put a smile on a customer's face and they'll want to come back.

Phil could hardly believe his ears as the payroll manager continued. 'If you had suggested to me a couple of years ago that I'd be doing this, I'd have thought you were crazy.' The man seemed to be reading his mind. 'And I gotta tell you that I really resented our director when she first took the position and started making all these changes but, surprisingly, I've grown to respect her as an outstanding leader. And I now actually look forward to occasionally escaping the pile of paperwork back at the office.'

Phil's need for a strategy, and his tired legs, told him to stay and talk some more, but Julie was eager to move on. She knew that koalas are smaller than a 10 cent piece at birth, and wanted to see how big they grew. He started to talk to her about it when another laugh from the kookaburra in the tree behind them drowned out his voice.

Julie laughed. 'Daddy, you've got a kookaburra's voice!'

Phil couldn't stop a smile. 'Kids remind us how important a smile is', Phil thought. 'And a laugh. How often do we have them at work? Not from the crude jokes on e-mail, which just waste time; or the public ridicule of some poor guy who's made a mistake. But genuine humour—the natural ability to laugh with others, rather than at others?'

Phil thought it through. By laughing at ourselves, we allowed others to relax a little and laugh with us—it was just a more mature way to be. This was especially true of management: a pretty grim bunch, overall. Work couldn't be one big joke that no-one took seriously, but good humour went a long way to creating a happier environment. And surely if staff were happier and felt better about working in an organisation, some of that goodwill must transfer to the customer.

A report in the weekend paper said laughter released natural chemicals in our bodies. These endorphins helped reduce tension and contributed to health and longevity, as well as the joy of feeling good.

'That's just what we want at work', thought Phil. 'If staff are able to put a smile on a customer's face, that must make the customer feel good. And then they'll want to do repeat business in that

50

happy environment. It doesn't matter if it's in our metal manufacturing or our financial services, our Australian or Asian branches; a smile will still bring customers back.'

Phil remembered his last business trip, where a flight attendant had created just such an experience. Phil had been running late, stressed as usual. As he reached the departure gate, he hurriedly asked the flight attendant: 'Is this New York?'

'Not yet sir', smiled the young man warmly. 'But it will be in two and a half hours.' Phil felt his body relax as they both laughed.

As he settled into his seat, he pulled the airline magazine from the seat pocket in front, and was casually reading it until he could use his laptop after takeoff. When the flight attendant arrived to take the drink order, Phil had the magazine open at a section on gourmet restaurants.

'If I were you, I wouldn't read that before you ate our food', said the attendant.

At first Phil was taken aback by the comment. The young man seemed to be denigrating his company's product. But because he had said it with a sparkle in his eye, Phil again burst into laughter, and knew he'd remember that human encounter long after he had forgotten the meal.

'Isn't that a pleasant change from the standard greeting you get from most people?' commented the man in the seat next to him. 'I'm sick of all that phoney have-a-nice-day chatter. It's about as plastic as the tray the food comes on.'

Phil smiled at the older white-haired gentleman, and the two of them started to chat about business. Phil and his fellow traveller agreed that their respective organisations would be a lot healthier if everyone had such a genuine and gentle sense of humour as the young flight attendant. Through his pleasant personality he had been able to put an unexpected smile on the face of two travel-weary customers.

> **Make your customers feel at home when you wish they were.**

Phil pointed out that the young flight attendant had epitomised a couple of age-old truths: 'A smile is a frown turned upside down', and 'Make your customers feel at home when you wish they were'.

The white-haired passenger laughed, and said he wished he'd thought of that. The two of them talked for most of the trip. Phil took the chance to try out a few customer service ideas he'd been thinking about. He'd learnt a lot just by having the chance to explain things.

'A bit of humour really made that service!' thought Phil, as Julie brought him back to earth with a yank on his hand.

Lion

A huge roar came from the adjacent enclosure: the king of the jungle prowled restlessly.

'That's scary, Dad.'

'Sounds just like my customers and my boss', joked Phil, forgetting who he was talking to. In his mind's eye he could see the sign his boss kept on his desk. It read:

Every morning a gazelle wakes up.
It knows it must run faster than the fastest lion
Or it will be killed.
Every morning a lion wakes up.

It knows it must outrun the slowest gazelle
Or it will starve to death.
It doesn't matter whether you're a lion or a gazelle.
When the sun comes up . . .
You'd better be running!

It was one of the rare things that he and his boss agreed on. Phil was already anxious to be up and running with his new service strategy; he wanted it all to happen on Monday morning.

One of the lions was licking between the pads of its paw.

'Look, Dad, maybe he's trying to get at a thorn', said Julie, 'just like in the story.'

Phil remembered reading it to her a year or so ago. A man finds a lion in pain from a thorn in its foot. He helps it, despite his fear, and pulls the thorn out. Years later the man finds himself in the lion's den, and the lion recognises him as the one who pulled a thorn from his infected paw—and so the man is spared. Phil remembered the moral of the story as being that if you help others with no thought of return, when you're thrown into the lion's den you'll probably be OK. 'After all, if you do the right thing by customers, most customers will do the right thing by you', he thought.

'The lion remembers if you treat it badly', Phil said out loud.

'Why would you want to do that?' Julie asked.

'Don't worry, Julie, I was talking to myself.'

'Customers remember good or bad experiences with your organisation too', Phil thought. It paid to see the long-term benefits of providing good service. Any customer, even an insignificant one, could grow into a powerful ally, with lots of future purchasing power. Everyone liked to feel that you valued them. And that you were interested in looking after them for a lifetime. Good service is when the customer comes back—and the goods don't!

Phil made a mental note to estimate the lifetime value of each customer. Even he was worth a lot to the coffee shop down the road, where he bought his $2 cappuccino each morning. Two dollars may not seem like much; but five days a week, for 48 weeks of the year, over a number of years, and it soon adds up. Customers aren't just one transaction, they're a long-term appreciating asset. A customer is like a lion: looked after now, it will pay off in the long run.

Phil knew that all of his products had a significantly higher price than a cup of coffee. And he knew that every employee had the ability to turn angry customers from lions to lambs by pulling out their proverbial thorns: by listening carefully, by not being defensive, and by taking positive action to fix the problem.

Phil found it staggering that more people in Western society die between 8 and 9 am on Monday morning than at any other time, while in the animal world deaths are evenly spread across the days. Was management by intimidation a contributing factor? Phil pictured his boss ranting and raving at staff about every customer complaint. He was determined to convince him that the customer service team would achieve better results if he could do precisely what his customer service representatives did—listen carefully rather than becoming aggressive or defensive.

> **No news is not necessarily good news. Loyal customers only occasionally take the time to complain.**

After all, most customer complaints were not directed at an individual. And there certainly was no reason for biting someone's head off for bringing a matter to the attention of management. If staff were treated badly for transmitting complaints, they would just stop doing it. 'We'd never get the information that way', he thought. And it was their most loyal customers who took the time to complain. No complaints wasn't necessarily positive—it could easily mean that customers couldn't be bothered, or had taken their business elsewhere. So no news was not necessarily good news.

'Wherever there's fear and conflict between management and employees, we should change it to cooperation', he thought. 'Treat staff or customers well and it pays off in the long run. Paul in pharmaceuticals is a good example. I should ask him. I've got a great set of ideas here. But how am I going to get anyone to listen? I'll talk about the first animal and they'll probably all switch off—or take off. Besides, all I've got is a few observations; I've got nothing to keep it all together.' He scribbled down a couple more notes on his ever-shrinking number of business cards.

'Except for the zoo itself, there's nothing that makes sense of what I've got', he said. 'This isn't likely to be a roaring success—I'll probably only get my head bitten off.'

'Daddy, are you all right?' asked Julie.

Phil thought people were starting to ask him that a little too often.

Mouse

As the pride of lions lounged peacefully, a small grey fieldmouse scampered in front of the enclosure. It was almost silent.

'Most customers are quiet as a mouse too', Phil thought. 'They never complain—even if they have reason to. Research says that 96.7% of unhappy customers never let out even a squeak of dissatisfaction to the organisation that has given them bad service. They may not tell us—but, boy, they tell everyone else. They roar it to all their friends and acquaintances. According to the research, unhappy customers will tell at least 15 other people, while satisfied ones will tell six at the most.[5] What's worse, what they say may not be accurate. They make their assessment on their perceptions alone.'

The customer may not always be right, but they are always the customer! 'We've got to make sure that the reality of our service is in line with the customers' expectations', thought Phil. Advertising set up customers' expectations, but how often was there a gap between what was promised and what was delivered? That could only annoy people.

> According to research, unhappy customers will tell at least 15 other people, while satisfied ones will tell six.

Only last week he'd stayed home to wait for a plumber who said he'd be there at 9 am and didn't arrive until nearly 11, with a long list of excuses about some emergency job. How much better if the tradesman had preset Phil's expectations by saying he would be there between 9 and 11 and then called with a progress report. And what about a couple of months ago, when he had phoned four locksmiths advertising a 24-hour service but got only an answerphone when he desperately needed a key at midnight?

He hated to admit it, but from time to time Candon had done that very thing—boasted about some service or feature so that customers would do business with them. There was always an argument over whether the claims were exaggerated, or premature, or whether the behind-the-scenes systems were in place to deliver them. Phil was a strong advocate of advertising, but some of the time the advertisements only annoyed customers and frustrated staff. Rather than overpromising and underdelivering, in the long term it'd be more effective to underpromise and overdeliver.

'It may be an advantage to be in the market-place first with a new product. But if the early bird gets the worm, surely the second mouse gets the cheese', thought Phil. 'Sometimes it's smarter to wait a little, and not make promises that might trap you later. Besides, it gives you more chances to exceed expectations.'

When it was time for the next campaign, Phil vowed not to get carried away by the hype and to speak up for his views like a man, not a mouse. He hoped he would keep his nerve and do the same thing for the service strategy on Monday—but would he have much to say?

Nit

'Dad, what's an animal smaller than a mouse?' asked Julie.

Phil couldn't immediately think of one, so with great parental skill he carefully steered Julie towards an explanation of the differences between animals and insects. 'I bet you can think of lots of insects that are smaller than a mouse.' His diversion tactics worked. Julie rattled off ants, bees, flies and mosquitoes.

'Good one, Jules. And there's heaps more. How about nits—the eggs of little bugs that live on other animals?'

'I don't care what you call them. I hate bugs, Dad. They're yucky.'

Phil thought of the equally annoying pests he had at work—including the projects he had to do over the weekend. He admitted to himself that he sometimes blew matters out of proportion, and treated problems more like a python strangling his food than the small, annoying pests they were at the time. But he also knew that it was often the 'little things' that could bite you if you didn't pay attention to detail.

Like details of how he was going to put all this together—something he was beginning to dread. Sunday, and the presentation Monday, were both looking grim. 'Yep, the details make the difference', Phil thought. He recalled reading about 'moments of truth'—a legendary phrase coined by Jan Carlzon, the CEO of Scandinavian Airlines in the mid-1980s. Carlzon turned the airline around from an $18 million loss to a $54 million profit in the space of a couple of years.

Carlzon attributed part of that success to moments of truth, which he defined as any encounter between a member of staff and a customer that lasted more than 15 seconds. Booking a ticket was a moment of truth. Checking your bags was a moment of truth. Getting a cup of coffee was another 15-second moment of truth. At that stage, the conventional wisdom was that the airline could increase profitability and market share if it improved its scheduling. 'Conventional wisdom. Yeah, right', thought Phil. He tried to remember the rest of the story.

Carlzon focused on scheduling, but recognised that there were many factors outside his control, like air traffic control and weather. Rather than try to improve scheduling by 100%, he aimed at improving 100 moments of truth by a tiny 1%. After all, it was much easier to achieve than a 100% improvement in scheduling.

> **Think big plans, but act on the small things.**

They found at Scandinavian Airlines that there were over 10 million moments of truth in a year. Carlzon encouraged all employees to do their bit . . . just a little bit better. That tactic was credited with turning the airline around at the time. After all, we all know it's easier to improve a little than to improve a lot. Carlzon succeeded by focusing everyone's efforts on their best, and on offering small suggestions for improvement. Phil wondered whether they had been able to sustain that approach or had slipped into complacency.

Phil could always relate to airline case studies, as he spent so much time on business travel. He recalled the astute garbage collector at Delta Airlines who noticed that very few passengers ever ate the garnish on their plates. When he had told management (and management was listening!), Delta cut out the lettuce and parsley and saved an amazing $1.5 million a year. All that garnish added was cost, not value, in the mind of the customer.

'Our business must have some things like that', thought Phil. 'All we've got to do is think about it.' He knew his firm had fallen into the trap of believing that more was better in terms of service. Yet, in his heart, he knew that only better was better. And that if an organisation focused on providing more and more services without knowing whether the customer appreciated them, it could only raise costs—without any increase in the customer's perception of value.

'Our management team gets bogged down with strategic plans and mission statements too often', thought Phil. 'They miss the little things that make the business tick. It's like the old Ethiopian proverb: *When spider webs unite, they can tie up a lion*. The big-picture stuff's essential but, come to think of it, we've never received a complaint about our mission statement.' Phil realised that all their complaints were about little things going wrong. It was important that his team think big plans but act on the small things.

Phil swatted a pesky fly from his face—another of those little annoyances. As the company's direction was clear, what management needed to do was to enlist the help of all employees to play a part in fixing the little things that bug customers. After all, Phil knew that for every customer that complained there were 24 who were equally unhappy but couldn't be bothered complaining.

'How often have I lain in bed at night and heard the annoying hum of a mosquito?' Phil thought. 'I know customers often cannot quite put their finger on some little annoyance, but they know it is bugging them.' If an organisation could only come up with the equivalent of a mosquito repellent to zap and eliminate the little annoyances, Phil thought some of the bigger issues would take care of themselves.

'Daddy, what are you thinking about?' asked Julie.

'Just some homework I've got to do.' Phil smiled at her. He vowed to stop thinking about it, and to stop worrying about how he'd work it out.

Ostrich

But as soon as they reached the ostriches, Phil started to worry again. 'I've got no theme, nothing central. How can I stand up in front of my peers with these kid's games?' he thought. He quickly jotted down the last few animals: joey jump high; kookaburra laugh; lion listen for the long term; mouse exceed expectations and get no squeaks.

Julie's face caught his attention. Her eyes were wide open at the largest bird she'd ever seen. 'Wow, Dad, it's even bigger than Big Bird on Sesame Street.'

The long neck of an ostrich towered above the fence. Surveying the enclosure, Phil noted that there was no sand, and wondered whether the birds really did bury their heads in it. 'Managers often bury their heads, especially with news they don't want to hear', thought Phil.

Only last week their managers had ignored a report on the competition prepared by a marketing trainee. They had paid lip-service to it, patronised the trainee, and dismissed his concerns as soon as he left the room. 'Ahhh, the enthusiasm of youth. He'll understand the realities better some day. He reminds me a bit of that other young feller we had some time back', said the sales manager.

> The six most expensive words in business: 'We've always done it that way'.

Phil remembered wanting to remind him that the 'young feller' had left to set up his own business, and had taken a major share of one of their most profitable product lines. Phil couldn't help but worry about the arrogance of the sales manager, who firmly believed that past success was a guarantee of success in the future. It was only because it had a good team that Candon was doing well. Phil reflected on other large organisations which had once been household names but weren't around any more. Like the ostrich, they'd buried their heads in the sand to the changes around them; and look where it got them.

Everything was more competitive. Phil remembered attending a seminar some time back where he'd been told that 46% of the Fortune 500 companies that existed in 1982 no longer existed in 1992! It really was survival of the fittest . . . and wisest! Too often, organisations weren't willing to evolve. Phil was firmly convinced that the six most expensive words in business were . . . 'We've always done it that way'.

'I'm stuck in this brainstorming thing, so I'd better make the most of it', Phil said out loud. He quickly looked about to make sure no-one had overheard him. The way things were going he'd be the one in the nursing home by the end of the weekend.

Phil sometimes wondered if he was too pessimistic, because he always felt the firm was vulnerable. Although he hoped he was wrong, he certainly didn't believe that they had an automatic right to dominate their markets—though some of his colleagues did. Certainly, he knew their solid record was one reason why many customers did business with them. But he also knew that a successful record can result in a dangerous level of complacency.

Success today did not guarantee your success tomorrow. He'd seen too many friends lose jobs to think otherwise. 'Unless organisations constantly adapt to changes in the environment, just like evolving animals, they're certain to become another endangered species', he thought.

Pig & Parrot

As they reached the wild boar pen, Phil was still thinking about how businesses had to be alert to change—being careful not to throw out the baby with the bath water. The snorting of the pigs reminded him of a story he thought Julie might like.

'I heard a man called Joel Barker talk about this on a video', he said:

A young man was driving along a country road in a fast red car. He was enjoying the drive when suddenly a car appeared round the corner, driving on the wrong side of the road. As the young man swerved to miss the car, he heard the woman driver yell: 'Pig!'

She shouldn't say that, the young man thought, because she was the one on the wrong side of the road. So he shouted back at her as he drove past: 'Cow!'

As he rounded the corner, he drove straight into a pig!

'I don't get it', said Julie.

Phil sighed. By the time he got this kid thing right, she'd be an adult.

Phil wanted to explain how Barker uses the story to show how people get stuck in patterns of thought. The way most people think when someone yells 'Pig!' it isn't helpful information. Barker says we have to be alert to how our environment changes, so that we don't react in the same old way in different situations. If he'd been able to tune in to the message and break his pattern, the young man could have avoided his accident. And how often in business do we have the equivalent of going around blind corners, with customers screaming warnings at us?

Pigs. Pigs might fly indeed. Phil pictured a pig with wings, flying around among the birds. His looked up the hill to the aviary, where parrots swooped and squawked, and smiled as he tried to visualise pigs dashing about and banging into the netting.

Maybe pigs could memorise words like parrots—just like half the customer service staff in the city. And their managers. Talk. Talk. Talk. All these compulsive imitators, who never uttered an original word. They seemed helplessly chained to their perch, only able occasionally to squawk some rote piece without any emotion whatsoever: 'Have a nice day', they'd say. 'Thank you for shopping here', they'd say. And they never meant it. The managers were worse: 'We've got to be customer-focused', 'We're a service organisation', 'The customer is king, the customer is king' . . . all words and no action.

> It's not just what you say to a customer, it's the way that you say it.

As Julie badgered him to go to the next enclosure, he thought of the time he had spent with his own father, and how he used to pick up on what Phil said. 'But Dad, I just said . . .' 'Son, it's not what you say. It's the way you say it!' If only he could say the same thing to his team today, so that they didn't mutter the words but actually offered sincere comments and solutions to the customers. If he could, Phil would remind them that parrot-like responses didn't make things better but worse. He knew that he wouldn't necessarily be popular for expressing his views, but someone had to do it.

'I just wish I had some way of saying it', he thought. 'Some way that would make sense of these animals, and be convincing, and simple. I can't just list 26 letters.'

Julie started chanting the alphabet song: 'A, B, C, D, E, F, G . . .'

'What letters go where?' thought Phil. 'Have any of them got something in common?' He pulled out the zoo map and looked at where they had been. A few animals had similar things to say, Phil noticed. But how should he group them?

A glimmer of hope lit the way to the next display.

Quokka

'Look Dad. Is it a miniature kangaroo or a really big rat?'

Phil was puzzled himself. He reread the sign, which informed him that the quokka was a small wallaby with a much shorter tail, which made it look like a rat.

The little creatures were best known for living on Rottnest Island, near Perth, Western Australia. An early Dutch explorer had so named the island because he thought it was a nest of rats. Now these same cute creatures provided a major tourist attraction as they roamed free.

'Years ago a nest of rats would be a turn-off', thought Phil. 'Times change. I can still remember my first PC. Didn't even have a hard disk. I wonder what the next technological change will be.'

Phil remembered a couple of articles on Internet trade: now virtually anyone could become an international retailer, even if they didn't have a traditional store, warehouse or product. Phil had read somewhere that one of Australia's largest retailers expected 5%–7% of its business to be on the Internet by the year 2000. That would be a turnover equivalent to opening two new department stores—without the overhead costs. Even an island country like Australia, with a small population a long way from anywhere, could make a lot of money from a previously distant world market.

'These global markets could be good news', thought Phil. On the other hand, even if Australia robbed sales from a retailer in New York, the reverse could just as easily occur. It would only add to competition for the consumer dollar.

'Things are hotting up', Phil thought. 'But then, if they're any good, maybe organisations could leap over traditional trade boundaries—as easily as the quokka might hop over my foot. With that sort of competition, underpromising and overdelivering would be even more important to get customers to come back. With global competition, you couldn't promise customers the world . . . and then give them an atlas! Customers have to come back like a boomerang', Phil thought. 'That's what we want to aim for.'

It cost five times more to obtain a new customer than to retain an existing one. Real success would come when all staff members realised they had to get customers to come back, so the business could enjoy the boomerang benefits of great customer service. Blaming or misusing technology wasn't going to do it for them. Nor was sticking their head in the sand about international competition. Phil knew it tied in with taking responsibility, with autonomy for customer service staff—with just about everything he had thought of while wandering around.

> It costs five times more to obtain a new customer than to retain an existing one.

'So where does this fit?' Phil asked himself. 'It's about changing how we look at our place in the world. It's about being aware of the unknown international competitor. It's about changing what we think and do. Yeah, that's it, it's about changing ourselves in order to change our service.'

Phil could see that a lot of his other ideas were about changing management behaviour and beliefs, and letting service follow from those changes. He reached around in his back pocket for the zoo map, hoping to find other animals that were examples of 'change yourself and service will follow'.

Rabbit

By the time Phil had gone through the map, ticking off the changes in management behaviour from the ape, the bear, the camel . . .

'No, dear, you can't keep him', the zookeeper said as Julie cuddled the little white rabbit.

Phil was aware how the cute little things could become a plague. If only his customer base would multiply a fraction so quickly! If statistics show that one happy customer tells six others, would those six tell six others, then 36 each tell six others, then . . .

Phil knew he was being overly optimistic, but

research had also shown that service leaders grow twice as fast as their competition.⁶ On Monday he'd remind his staff to hop to it and consistently meet and exceed their customers' needs. They just had to treat each customer not as a one-time transaction but as a long-term, appreciating asset. 'Those positive attitudes are always contagious', he thought. 'And negativity always fuels further negativity. Whatever we do, we've got to be positive about it.'

He hated the word 'no', wherever he heard it. From his boss or his staff or, most of all, when a supplier said it to him, when Phil himself was a customer. Only last year he had needed to build a new garage and wanted to withdraw some money from two term deposits. When he called the first bank, the woman told him: 'No you can't. Don't you realise it's a term deposit, dummy?' She didn't actually call him a dummy, but her tone of voice implied that that was what she thought—for his being impertinent enough to want to break the rules.

The woman at the second bank had a totally different attitude. 'Yes, certainly, sir. We'd be happy to help, but do you realise that, because it is a term deposit, you'll lose some interest?' Phil said it was OK, and she processed the transaction without any fuss. When he called the first bank back another customer service operator told him that he could, in fact, have done the same thing.

'Why the %^&$# was I told that I couldn't?' thought Phil. When the time came to redeposit the funds he put them all in the second bank, where the staff had immediately seen a way to say 'yes', rather than a justification to say 'no'. 'I can see what the boss is going to say to all this—"no"', thought Phil. But, as Tom Peters said, service was spreading like an epidemic; and if organisations didn't catch it, they would surely perish. 'We say "yes" at Candon', Phil thought. 'Maybe that's why we're doing well. Maybe anything creates a success that builds on itself. As with rabbits, success breeds success!'

> **Find a way to say 'yes', rather than a justification for saying 'no'.**

Phil's eyes moved from the rabbit in Julie's arms to the map in his hands. 'How can saying "yes" fit with the other things I've worked out? What goes with the rabbit?' Nothing jumped out. It was just a basic customer service principle, he thought—multiply your customer base, find a way to say 'yes'. But then so was the idea of horses for courses; so was the idea of jumping as high as customers ask you to.

Phil started to skim, looking for basic service principles across his now-crumpled map. 'AHA!' he yelled, finding another one at the parrots—be sincere.

Julie, and everyone else, was miles away.

78

Clutching the map in his hand, he jogged off after her. It was beginning to look like he would be pulling the proverbial rabbit from the hat on Monday. A few more ways of grouping his ideas, and he'd actually have a strategy.

Seal & Starfish

Julie was watching feeding time at the seals. As she squealed with delight, Phil squirmed a little, remembering the pair of sealskin boots he used to wear, long before the public outrage about clubbing the little things to death. Now he wouldn't be seen dead in a pair.

'Seals are cute', Phil thought. 'Funny how they move so well in water and are so clumsy on land. I wonder how they train them?' Phil's thoughts wandered as he and Julie looked for a seat.

When he was growing up in Minnesota, most kids in the neighbourhood wore sealskin boots in winter. No-one even thought of how they had been produced. Funny how values change, he thought. Now everyone was conscious of the environment.

Organisations today had to take account not only of the economics of business, but also of the environmental, ethical and social effects.

His hours of reading were starting to pay off. He remembered more research—this time indicating that customers were more likely to support organisations that acted in accordance with the individual's own belief system, even if that meant paying a premium price. Phil didn't kid himself that business should exist for altruism alone, and had no silly idea that this view would be accepted overnight. But he felt it was important to at least start raising the corporate consciousness about the public conscience. Hey, even the zoo recycled animal waste and sold it to garden shops as a unique range of 'zoo pooh' fertilizer. He wouldn't mind hiring the person who thought of that on his marketing team.

From seals he moved to an old story of starfish. Thousands had once been washed up on a beach, destined to die as the tide went out. One man walked along and threw some back into the water. An onlooker commented: 'Can't you see there are thousands, and that what you're doing won't make any difference?' Undeterred, the man casually tossed another starfish back into the sea and commented: 'It made a difference to that one.'

Admittedly, Phil was more of an economist than

an environmentalist. But different parts of Candon controlled precious resources, and it made good economic sense to do the right thing, and to match the public perception of the right thing. Even without resources, the pharmaceutical arm had to take ethics really seriously.

Thirty years ago there were no negative perceptions about sealskin boots, he thought. You just needed to be tuned into the ever-evolving marketplace. If you did what was right and did the right thing by your team, customers and community, they were more likely to do the right thing by you. Like the ball on the nose of the seal, it was a finely tuned balancing act between pure economics, ethics and the environment.

> Organisations have to take account not only of the economics of business, but also of the environmental, ethical and social effects.

As he sat in the seal amphitheatre, Phil unrolled his map and looked for matching ideas. 'It's about investing some trust in the values of your team and community', he thought. 'What other of my ideas say the same thing?'

He quickly gave up as a headache took over. As he caught up to Julie she waved to the camel she had seen before. 'The reservoir of ideas!' he thought. 'Trusting your people's ideas. And the dingo—create trust and people will take responsibility. This trust idea is definitely going to be part of the strategy.'

Tiger

After every meeting a former boss of Phil's used to say: 'Go kill 'em, tiger.'

Any idiot knew that customers didn't want to be killed! Nor did they want to feel as if they were prey to some marauding salesperson stalking them relentlessly.

It used to be that closing a sale was the only thing, thought Phil. Like a tiger would go for the kill. But nowadays Phil was wise enough to recognise that customers expected something different. He knew that his long-term success did not depend on closing a sale but on opening a rela-

tionship. Success came from turning one-time customers into repeat business—into loyal advocates.
It was the boomerang idea again. As it cost more
to attain a new customer than to retain an existing
one, they should look after the existing customer
long after the sale had been closed.

Phil had also learned by painful experience that
it takes months to find a customer and only seconds to lose one; not unlike a tiger who misses a
meal by moving too quickly
and frightening its prey.

Phil read the plaque while
Julie pressed against the
glass. 'The Siberian tiger,
the largest living cat in the
world, is becoming increasingly rare in the wild', it
said. He wondered whether
that was due to humans, or whether it was the
animal's inability to adapt to changes in its habitat.
Many once-great corporations were extinct for the
same reason, like the buggy whip when the car
was introduced.

> **Long-term success
> depends not on closing
> a sale, but on opening
> a relationship.**

What was that old saying about a leopard not
changing its spots? Surely the same applied if a
tiger was unable to change its stripes? Change
waited for no animal—or man. Any company that
didn't focus on relationships wouldn't be around
to go for the kill. And staff relationships were as
important as customer ones. After all, a job was a
relationship. Looking at it that way, it was man-

agement's job to build the best environment and relationship it could.

Looking around the zoo, Phil was happy to see the animals weren't in tiny cages any more but had much larger and more natural enclosures. They seemed healthier. They were certainly more fun to look at. Still, it'd be much better if they could roam free. But then millions of children like Julie would never be able to experience the thrill of seeing such a variety of awesome animals. 'What simple changes would make our working habitat a more pleasing environment?' he asked himself. 'How can we make it better in the long term for both customers and staff?'

Changing stripes was always difficult. Some middle management had even resisted installing a filtered water-cooler the previous year because they had always drunk coffee. They couldn't understand why employees wanted a watering hole. In fact, a few objected on the basis of cost, which seemed like penny-pinching to Phil. Even old Smithers had vehemently objected to it: 'We never had one before and we got along just fine.'

Good relations with staff paid in the long run. So, too, did good customer service. And the better you could meet the needs and wants of your staff, within reason, the more likely they were to meet the needs and wants of your customers. Phil resolved to ask employees for other suggestions for making work more comfortable. After all, happy employees yielded happier customers. 'A good and

flexible environment, and a good, flexible relationship is what's behind great service', he thought.

Phil knew that there was no time like the
present to install good habits in your habitat. And
management had to take the first step towards
changing relationships.

He took out his last business card. He'd have
to miss the last few letters, but he squeezed in as
much as he could: ostrich: head out of sand;
parrot: don't mimic; quokka: international; rabbit:
say 'yes' to success; seal: balance. That was it. The
rest he'd have to remember.

Unicorn

Smithers was the typical organisational dinosaur. Phil had no doubts that such prehistoric animals had once roamed the earth, but he didn't need a two-legged one in his department today!

'Julie is probably the only kid in the street that doesn't like dinosaurs', Phil thought. 'Horses and unicorns are more her thing.'

Phil knew there hadn't been a creature called a unicorn, with the body of a horse and a single horn like a rhinoceros. He hadn't gotten around to telling Julie that, though. And, after all, you couldn't always explain things scientifically. Who knows? Maybe unicorns had once existed. Maybe they were related to the modern horse or rhinoceros, or had evolved from them. Evolution was coming up a lot today.

Phil saw an ad for a chocolate, and his mouth watered at the image. 'I'm a sucker for advertising', he thought. He decided on a sugar fix, just to boost his energy. The trip round the zoo was nearing its end, and Julie had thoroughly exhausted him.

The chocolate cost 20% more than in the supermarket, but Phil didn't care. As his teeth sunk into it, the cost was miles from his thoughts. He had willingly paid for the convenience of having it available when he wanted it, the way he wanted it—cold and firm. People paid more for exactly what they needed. Julie had started chatting to another child, so he let his mind wander. His first job had been stacking chocolates and other goods in a supermarket. He knew his kids wouldn't even recognise how he used to work. He'd put price tags on each item, done manual stocktakes, and used carbon paper to record orders. There weren't any 'use by' dates on packages. At the checkout counter customers had waited while he keyed in individual prices. When he was 17 it was a different world.

He was glad the scanners had made the queues much faster. 'We all take it for granted that the scanning is accurate, and that we can pay with credit cards', he thought. 'And we can take extra cash home with our groceries.' His grandfather wouldn't have believed it.

Unlike Smithers, Phil knew that technology had made customer service better than ever. He also knew that the best service strategy was to use the latest in technology without losing the personal touch. Like the hotel which had the phonetic pronunciation of Phil's name on its computer and had a database record of when he had last visited,

> The best service strategy is to use the latest technology without losing the personal touch.

which enabled the receptionist to then cheerfully greet him with a 'Welcome back, Mr Wilenski'.

The last time he was at a supermarket it was clear that they hadn't learnt that lesson. The cashier was particularly grumpy and rude. When he commented on her attitude, and pointed out that she could at least say thank you for his business, she snarled: 'I don't need to say thank you—it's printed on the back of your docket!'

Phil had met that sort of attitude before. He also knew that it might not matter so much when people started shopping from a home terminal. But many would still go to stores to see and touch the products, and to interact with others. People search for a balance between 'high tech' and 'high touch'. These days, high tech was a given—like the money you needed to get into a card game at a casino—but there were no guarantees of winning unless you played your cards well. And, an MIT study showed that 80% of technological innovations actually came from customers.[7]

Smithers' day was past. If he wasn't careful, there wouldn't be any jobs for him unless he learned new survival skills. The tools that Smithers had used as a trainee were already antiquated, confined as relics to some industrial museum: replaced by faxes, photocopiers, computers, mobile phones, e-mail and who knows what next—virtual reality? What impact would that have on the marketplace? Would children get the same joy from going to the zoo, or would they prefer the experience of a virtual world? A world that might include the sensation of riding a camel in the Sahara, tracking an elephant through the jungle, or wrestling a crocodile.

Phil came back to reality as Julie yanked his hand again: 'Dad, I gotta go to the bathroom.'

'Are you OK to go by yourself, Princess?'

A female passer-by overheard and volunteered to help. When he thanked her for her unsolicited kindness, she cheerily replied: 'My pleasure . . . What are we here for if we can't help each other a little along the way?'

And what impact would the new technology have on attitudes towards service? Phil wondered whether he'd ever again have to listen to the feeble excuse: 'It's the computer's fault'.

Or would it become an even more common excuse? He cringed whenever he heard it. Usually he'd say: 'A computer is simply a business tool, like a hammer. If the hammer misses the nail, and hits you on the thumb, whose fault is it . . . the operator's or the hammer's?' Phil could almost see the staff in his local bank ducking behind the counter when he approached, he'd told it to them so many times.

'Technology only helps service if we remember that service is delivered by people', he thought. 'If we remember that, perhaps the phrase "it's the computer's fault" will become an endangered excuse. He'd no longer receive advertising letters that claimed he was a valuable customer but had his name spelled incorrectly. He wondered whether one day he'd also succumb to living in the past, if he lost track of technology and what it could offer. Smithers was a smart man. It made Phil realise that he should enjoy every day, because whatever complaints he might have, these were the good old days he might long for in the future.

Phil also knew that nobody could head into the future if they weren't pointed in a forward direction. 'We can't look back to the way things were done. We can't deny technology. We've got to use it to the optimum and make it work', Phil thought.

Another basic principle. It would make sense for the company to look at all of them again. With a bit of luck, that's what Phil's strategy would get them to do.

Vulture

'Yuck Dad . . . they look scary.' Julie's grip tightened on Phil's hand as they passed the vultures. 'I don't wanna hang around here long.'

'OK, darling', agreed Phil. He couldn't help but think of the competition, as he went eyeball to eyeball with one of the scavengers. 'They just circle around and wait for someone else to do all the work, and then eat the spoils', he mumbled.

'I don't care, Dad. Let's go.'

Phil was still thinking about the potential customers they'd wooed for ages, who then, after one little slip-up, had gone to the competition. He thought it was unfair, yet he knew in his heart of hearts that if you didn't look after your customers, someone else would—the vultures. Although cursing the poachers, he was painfully aware that too often departmental managers were to blame, through fighting over budgets or territory. He could even see it in himself.

'If I'm guilty, then I have to change too', he thought. 'There are a lot of changes I have to make to myself, starting with being more positive. We managers have to get our own house in order before we give staff a hard time!' After all, a person only had so much energy—and it

> **If you don't look after your customers, someone else will . . .**

seemed futile for him and his colleagues to waste their energy fighting among themselves for the company's limited resources when the real threat lay with their competitors outside.

There was a sign on the enclosure: 'Keep fingers clear!' Phil knew the sign he needed at work: 'Keep all the vultures outside, and forget that at your peril'.

'This has to be one of the first things to do', thought Phil. 'As a team we have to make a step somewhere towards all the other principles I've been thinking about. Put things into action. Whatever strategy I come up with, it has to include that.'

Whale

Like Julie, Phil hadn't liked the vultures much, and his breathing slowed as they reached the huge whale pool. As large as it was, it seemed unfair to limit two of the largest mammals on earth to such a confined space.

Whale-watching had spawned a new tourist industry. Where once only men carrying harpoons would be excited about seeing a whale, now it was families carrying cameras.

Last April Phil had taken the family on a whale-watch cruise in Hawaii, which offered a money-back guarantee if there wasn't a sighting. It was near the end of the season, and Phil had missed out on seeing one. Although the tour operator had given everyone a voucher for another whale-watching cruise, there was no way Phil could make the time. He guessed that hardly anyone else would be able to take advantage of the offer, either. Still, the gesture was a good marketing tool—it encouraged people to book, and it created goodwill. Everyone recognised that the tour operator had no control over the migratory patterns of the whales.

You'd have to be pretty confident before offering a guarantee, thought Phil. Otherwise it could be a recipe for disaster. But if your competitors already offered one it could be disastrous not to. Phil reckoned that a voucher for another cruise, rather than a complete refund, was pretty fair.

Recently he'd visited a couple of restaurants where the food was second-rate and he had complained. At one restaurant the manager had deducted the cost of the meal from his bill. Although Phil was partly satisfied he didn't go back because the experience had left a bad taste in his mouth. At the other restaurant the manager had apologised, offered a partial refund, and a voucher for the equivalent of that course. Phil thought the second approach was better business. First, it got the customer to come back and have another, perhaps more pleasant experience. And the customer would probably spend more than the cost of the voucher. Second, it reduced the likelihood of a customer complaining merely to get a free meal.

'Wow, they're big, Dad. Remember when we went on that boat in Hawaii and I threw up?'

'Funny how we're recalling the same experience from a different perspective', Phil thought.

'Today, I didn't get sick with the fairy floss like you said I would.' She grinned cheekily. 'So can we stay and see them do some tricks? Please, Dad. Please!'

It was only a 10-minute wait till the next show. Phil happily agreed and they found a seat in the stand nearby.

'How come, if they're an animal, they can breathe under water? Where do they go to sleep? How can you tell if it's a boy or a girl whale? How can they float if they weigh so much? Will we get wet if they sneeze? How did they teach it to jump through that hoop?'

Phil couldn't wait for the show to begin so the endless barrage of questions would stop—although he hoped she kept that sort of curiosity through her life. 'I'm not really sure how they do all that', said Phil.

The man sitting beside them spoke up: 'Someone told me that once they capture a whale, they let it settle in for a while and get comfortable. Then they start training it by giving it fish when it swims over a rope on the bottom of the pool. The whale soon learns that this is safe and easy, and keeps doing it to get the fish. After a while they move the rope higher up, so the whale learns that it only gets the fish when it swims over the

96

rope. Gradually they move the rope higher and higher, until it's out of the water. Then the whale needs to jump over the rope to get the fish. Finally they take the rope away, and the whale jumps without it. That's how you get whales to jump. Simple, isn't it?' He looked pleased with himself.

'I only wish it were that simple to train staff', Phil joked.

'It is!' replied his new friend, who introduced himself as Ken Blanchard, the management guru. 'It's very similar to training whales. You can't expect them to perform new tasks immediately. But give them small tasks and reward them as they achieve these. Then stretch them by "raising the rope"—raising the standards.' He continued, chuckling to himself: 'You don't think that the zoo has any extraordinary recruitment strategies, do you? They just get an ordinary, healthy whale and teach it to be a performing star, all through a system of rewards. People are a little more complex, but the principle remains the same.'

Phil saw the truth in what he said. Many times he'd seen new employees thrown in at the deep end, without getting any training or feedback. 'But how should we set up rewards and punishments?' he asked himself. Phil had always felt that the carrot worked better than the stick, but he also knew that there were some employees who were never likely to contribute.

It was better to turn them loose, he thought. After all, the whale trainer probably couldn't afford to keep feeding non-performing whales in some tank out the back. Especially if they weren't adding any value for the customer. They'd just have to get new whales if the ones they had couldn't do the job. 'Yep, sometimes it's easier to change whales than change people', Phil decided.

Beside him Ken continued: 'It's important with staff that you celebrate the little successes along the way towards completing a big project, rather than waiting until the task is finished. If we don't do that, it would be like playing in a football game when no-one in the audience cheered as each goal was scored. Can you imagine the frustration if there was no cheering until the final whistle blew?'

'You're absolutely right', replied Phil. 'And do you know what the two most under-utilised words in business are these days?'

While Ken was thinking of a clever answer, Julie piped up: 'Thank you!'

Phil stopped in surprise at her reply. He hadn't thought she was at all interested in the conversation. She wasn't.

'Thanks for taking me to the zoo, Dad', she said, snuggling his side. She was starting to get tired.

'Smart little girl, there', said Ken. 'She's absolutely right.'

Phil smiled. 'We've spent years teaching Julie

how to say thank you', he thought. 'It's only now that I'm learning that's what I've got to do at work—not just because it's right, but because it's good business too. It's the way people learn; it builds strong relationships and makes for more trust, autonomy and respect.' It was all starting to fit.

X-breed

Both the alphabet and Phil were nearly exhausted. His head was spinning with a multitude of strategies and operations. There were almost as many ideas as animals, and it was impossible to implement them all. But a few basic ideas were starting to gel.

'We've got to go back to the basics of service—that's half of what I've worked out today', he thought. 'And dealing with change, I've thought a lot about dealing with change. Trust, too. Does that cover all the animals?'

He couldn't cover all of them. What worked for

one animal might be the downfall of another. After all, a duck's webbed feet were pretty effective in a pond, but not much use to a rabbit on open pasture. Phil remembered that he had to consider 'horses for courses'. Good managers knew how to hire square

Take the best of the best, and make it yours.

pegs and put them in square holes—and round pegs in round holes too. That way they made the most out of people.

'It's exactly the same for Candon', Phil thought. 'We depend on taking the best practices from everyone, from a cross-section of organisations, and adapting them to what we need. We've got so many different divisions we have to use every resource. We've got to learn from the best, and make it ours.' He was certain that by taking the best of each breed—the best of the best—they would be able to form a perfect hybrid. 'If we don't, we won't survive', he thought. 'We've got to be flexible.'

Julie's feet were dragging, so they didn't stop long. Phil stood daydreaming for a second; just long enough to remember that only three of the Fortune 500 companies from 1900 still existed, without merger or acquisition. He knew his task wouldn't be easy, but it would be essential to avoid corporate extinction. After all, the only time that success came before work was in the dictionary!

Yak

As he bundled Julie in his arms, heading for the carpark, Phil felt like a yak. A strong, reliable beast of burden. It certainly wasn't a glamour animal but it was one that could always be relied on to carry the load. That's what a good parent was. 'So are many of our employees, who do their jobs faithfully day in and day out', thought Phil.

Come to think of it, Phil sometimes felt a bit that way himself, not only at work but at home. He didn't resent it. In fact, he prided himself on his reliability and liked to think that others could call on him to help with their load. But every now and then he wished he could relinquish the role and have someone say: 'Relax. You don't need to worry about that any more. Everything will be all right.'

If he was honest with himself, sometimes he just wanted to let go of the responsibility. Like Julie today, he thought. He smiled at the look of total contentment on Julie's face as she rested in his arms. But being a beast of burden, permanently trying to be the perfect father and perfect manager, to create the perfect organisation . . . it just didn't seem possible.

> You can't take care of your customers, staff or family, if you don't take care of yourself.

Phil had never seen a yak, and he couldn't help but wonder whether anyone had ever seen the perfect organisation. Maybe he could relax a little if he accepted that Candon would never reach perfection. 'We can keep high standards of excellence, but still relax and let go of the little imperfections', thought Phil. Even at home. Especially at home.

He vowed to let himself off the hook for what he hadn't got done at the end of each week. And to give himself a pat on the back for all that he *had* managed to achieve. He was determined to focus more on what went right each day, rather than on what went wrong. He resolved to do whatever he could to reduce his current level of stress. 'After all, you can't take care of your customers, staff or family if you don't take care of yourself', he thought. 'I'll be no good to anyone if I end up in hospital . . . or worse.'

But another voice inside his head nagged: 'I'm too busy to exercise. I never seem to have enough time for my family and friends. Who can spare an hour to go to the gym? How can I quietly read a book and listen to music when I've got so much to think about? And as for a massage, you've got to be kidding!' Phil pushed those thoughts away.

No, the customer was not number one! It finally dawned on him that nothing was as important as his personal wellbeing. He knew that this sounded the opposite of popular business thinking. But he could never give of his best unless he was healthy—both physically and mentally.

His thoughts wandered as he did likewise around the carpark, trying to remember where he had left the car . . . 'I need to be at my personal best to give my personal best. If I'm at work and feeling guilty about yelling at the kids or not calling my parents, or resentful that I had to give up a golf game to work on customer service strategy all weekend, what frame of mind will I be in to greet my customers? I need to have my own batteries recharged. I've forgotten how good it feels to be well. From now on, I'm going to get at least a little exercise every day', he thought.

He was puffing as he set Julie down next to the car. Phil had no grandiose plans to go on massive Himalayan treks, but he knew his day-to-day journey would be more pleasant. He knew he could never be perfect. He also knew that doing his best was the best he could do.

'Monday's going to be pretty good', he thought.

Zebra

Phil still wanted to get his strategy right. 'I'm on the way, I'm on the way', he said to himself as he unlocked the car. 'I feel like I've lost weight', he said to Julie.

'Great, Dad.' She had hardly heard the words.

Because of his new resolution, Phil wasn't even concerned that they had missed seeing the zebras. He'd brainstormed ahead and was pretty proud of himself: an idea without even seeing the animal! And it was a good idea.

Few customer or employee situations were ever black or white: there was usually a grey area, not like on those beautiful beasts. And no two zebras had the same clearly defined stripes. Like customers and employees, each was an individual; each with their own unique characteristics; each requiring an adaptable response. Guidelines were useful, but the most valuable skill any manager could have was to be able to combine knowledge with the instinct for doing the right thing at the right time.

'The zoo wasn't the boring trip I'd expected', thought Phil. 'It gave me a new perspective, on service and on myself. Management is much simpler than people think.'

Julie was sound asleep before Phil had finished fastening her seatbelt. He noticed his own fatigue as he sat in front of the wheel.

> **Few customer problems are ever black or white.**

'I could do with a few ZZZZs myself', he thought. He clicked his seatbelt into place. As he stared through the windscreen, the last piece of the puzzle clicked too. Phil saw the final strategy— four overriding ideas he could take from all his animal inspirations:

☆ revisit basic service principles

☆ set your management and staff up for change

☆ trust in your team and customers

☆ actually start making the changes to get the principles happening

He ticked them off on his fingers.

'Are you all right?' asked the woman getting into the car next to his.

'Yes, thank you', he said. He was too happy to be embarrassed, as he turned on the ignition and started humming along to the music. He smiled at a break in programming when the DJ's dulcet tones interrupted and asked for audience feedback on the top tunes: 'We listen to you because you listen to us.'

A new beginning

'You can't drive into the future if you're looking into a rear vision mirror', thought Phil. He turned the car into the driveway, almost hitting Karen's sedan. 'She's not supposed to be home until tomorrow night', he thought. 'What's happened?'

Fearing the worst, Phil quickly bundled the sleeping Julie into his arms. He licked the remnants of fairy floss from her hands absentmindedly. 'What's happened?' he asked Karen as he opened the door.

'Mum's much better. She's sleeping OK, and the doctors said there was nothing I could do, so I came home. I know you've had a tough week, so I thought I'd be here with the kids over the weekend.'

Phil felt guilty about being annoyed with her earlier. 'When I get stressed at work I can be so insensitive', he thought. 'I forget how much they mean to me. After all, they're why I work the long hours in the first place.' Customer service strategies could come and go, but his family was always there for him. And if he didn't devote enough time to the people he cared most about, he wouldn't be good for his staff or his customers.

'I love you, honey', he sighed, as he gave his wife a hug.

'Oh, what do you want?' she joked. 'You haven't said that for ages.'

'Yeah, I know. But I do love you.'

'It's still nice to hear. I wish you'd tell me what you're thinking more often.'

Phil wished his boss would do the same.

'Phil, by the way, Alan left a message on the answering machine while you were out. They're playing golf again tomorrow. Why don't you go? It'd be good for you to relax a little. I was going to call him back, but I knew that you had that customer service project to work on.'

'Oh, I've almost finished that. I did most of it at the zoo and just need about an hour to bring it together.'

'Great!' She knew better than to ask any more questions when he was in one of those vague moods.

'I'll tell you about it some time—it's pretty interesting—but right now I just want to unwind and be with you.'

Monday morning

'How's the customer service strategy coming along, Phil—finished yet?' his boss asked as Phil's turn to present came.

'Sure is', said Phil as he stood up. 'On Saturday I had a great day at the zoo and I suddenly realised that customer service is kinda like being a giraffe.'

Puzzled faces looked at him. 'Poor guy's been working too hard', thought his boss. With those looks, Phil knew he was sticking his neck out further than any giraffe.

He set up where he was going: 'Look, I know what you're thinking, and admittedly this sounds a bit bizarre, but if you hang in there with me, I guarantee this is a great idea. It's not fluffy, it'll boost our bottom line, and it's a great way of supporting our staff morale.'

'Here's what I want to do', said Phil. 'I want us to develop a strategy that will work. Now, we all know that we can come up with strategies pretty easily—we have before—but getting them to work long-term is pretty hard.' Phil smiled as every single person there nodded. 'So, we need to do something different. Right?' Again the nods. Phil felt he had them with him.

He kicked off the idea of animal analogies. He explained how they'd be easy to remember, how they'd be great symbols for different customer service values, how people could identify with one animal or another, how they could use them in training, and how they covered the whole range of service issues. And how they, too, could evolve as circumstances changed.

'Now, I don't have time to cover the analogies for every single animal. But there are some over-riding groups of ideas that can act as a guide to the animals.' Phil paused. No smiles. No nodding. But no coughs or paper-shuffling either.

'There are four broad categories to the strategy. The first is to revisit all the basic service principles, the ones we think we know but never do. The second is that we in management, as well as our staff, commit to changing ourselves in ways that support service.' The nods were coming back.

'Third, we in management have to trust and

empower our team and our customers. Lastly, we have to act. This is the supertough one. We have to make decisions and make them fast. And we have to evolve to meet the changing market and the changing customer.'

'So far so good', thought Phil. But he was worried that he didn't have all the trimmings for his presentation. No statistics. No tables. The only orthodox thing he had was an executive summary, and it would have to do. He gave a quick rundown of 10 or 12 of the letters and how they worked. They seemed to listen, but Phil still wasn't sure whether they were truly with him.

He moved on to each part of the strategy in turn. He gave a few examples of revisiting basic service principles, using good old-fashioned horse sense. He told the story of the plastic-wrapped fish and the fish on the ice. 'What that tells us', he said, 'is that customer perceptions are reality, and we'd better deal with them. Other stories can show us the importance of treating people as individuals, and learning from our mistakes.' Phil told them about the stablehand, and the ponies of different sizes and temperaments.

Phil quickly passed through the importance of little annoyances, and how nits were a perfect metaphor. And how, by saying 'yes', success would breed like rabbits. Or that the tiger sales mentality was no longer a long-term option in the new economy. 'Even the mouse shows us that we need to underpromise and overdeliver', he said. 'These are just a sample of what the animal metaphors tell us about service principles. Even the joey supports the idea of our giving customers the service they want, by asking "How high?" when they ask us to jump!'

The team was starting to come with him.

Phil started off the next step—changing themselves. 'The simplest one here is the ape. We simply have to lead by example, because whatever we do, everyone sees and follows. That means we have to change—to change the company. And the same is true of most of customer service.' He caught a few frowns, so he explained.

'Look, we've got to find out what's really going on with our customers: and not hibernate like the bear. We've got to focus on external competitive vultures, not our in-house politics: like the camel-committee. We've got to change our culture so we set high standards, we listen to staff and customers, and have a laugh doing it: that's the giraffe, the lion, the kookaburra. As management, much of the responsibility for customer service rests with us. That's what these animal analogies are saying.'

Phil added that they couldn't leave their heads in the sand like the ostrich, that they had to monitor the environment and change with it. And that they had to get pointed in the right direction like the unicorn, set a direction and embrace the benefits of technology. From there they could get the balance of the seal, and gain the ability to see shades of grey that the zebra couldn't—and even

114

learn the self-acceptance of the hardworking yak, which doesn't need to be perfect.

As Phil spoke he became even more animated, the excitement and fun of creating the strategy taking over his presentation. He monitored the boss and the team as he spoke, and towards the end could sense that all these animals were confusing them.

'It's simple', he said. 'Take the next idea of empowering staff and customers. Through the metaphor of the dingo we can see how we can develop trust by consistently treating people with care and reward. That trust is the basis for great service, because great service requires that staff be willing to make decisions. The story of the elephant shows that we have to help staff break through all the rules they may have in order to give great service. And if we teach staff the skills, they'll be right for their working life, just as if we had taught them to fish. It's the same idea as using reward to change and train people, which is what I talked about with the whale.'

'But all this is pointless if we don't do something. And that's the message from the last overall strategy. The impala monitors the environment and changes the instant there's a problem. The elephant breaks free when there is urgency in the environment. The giraffe is all about sticking its neck out—taking a risk. And the vulture highlights that we have to work together as a management team, and as a service team, to face all challenges. Action is what counts, and it's up to us to act, to come up with our own unique blend for success which, like rabbits, will breed further success.'

Phil reiterated his plan of action: 'At both management and frontline levels we have to look at the principles, the responsibility, the trust, and the commitment to act.' Phil paused, breathed out, and waited for a comment. None came, so he decided to go the whole hog.

'Oh yeah, and one more thing', he added. 'I'll be using some of my accrued holidays to take the family away next month. I know it's budget time, but my team has it under control, and there's nothing else I can add to this customer service strategy. After all, we can't take care of our customers if we don't take care of ourselves! And remember: the best customer relations is to never treat your customers like you treat your relations! . . . That is, don't take them for granted until it's too late.'

No-one spoke. Phil wondered whether he'd pushed the boundary too far. But there was no turning back.

Silence. Then, his boss spoke slowly: 'Phil, we shouldn't even treat our relations like we treat our relations. We should be telling people we love that we love them—that we care about them. Because if you're not happy at home, you can't be happy at work, and the customers will pick up on that.'

Love?! His boss had used the 'L' word! In all his years in business Phil had never heard that word. 'Maybe things are changing; maybe we are thinking differently', he thought.

Before he had had much time to reflect on this thought, the HR director commented: 'I thought you'd lost your mind when you started your presentation, but I now think your animal analogies make some sense. I don't agree with them all, but there is some solid stuff there. And let's face it, over a drink on a Friday night, who hasn't said that work was a zoo?'

A murmur of agreement and quiet laughs rose from the table. Small conversations started up, talking about the animals and who was which.

Phil overheard the finance director joking: 'Yeah, and animals are suing for defamation at being compared with the average worker!' she said.

Laughter ran round the table, breaking the tension remaining from Phil's presentation. Phil heard the legal director laugh at something the company secretary had said. The level of energy buzzing around the meeting room amazed him. It was all very strange.

The presentation had gone much better than Phil could ever have expected, and his little sojourn to the zoo hadn't been a waste of time after all. He remembered that in Africa, to go on *safari*, the Swahili word for journey, means to leave the comfort of civilisation to venture into the wild. Phil had definitely ventured well and truly outside his comfort zone at the beginning of his presentation, but no longer felt he was a lone voice in the wilderness with his unorthodox but eco-logical views on customer service.

Ape

Monkey see . . . monkey do. Lead by example.

Bear

Get management out of hibernation to reduce complaints.

Camel

Remember that the competition is external.

Dingo

You can teach an old dog new tricks if you create a climate of trust.

Elephant

You're only strong if you feel empowered.

Fish

Teach your staff to fish and you'll eat for a lifetime.

Giraffe

Stick your neck out to set higher standards.

Horse

Good service is plain horse sense.

Impala

Change direction quickly to save your life.

Joey

When the customer says jump, ask how high.

Kookaburra

Share a laugh and build your business.

Lion

Turn angry customers from lions to lambs.

Mouse

Stop customers squeaking by exceeding their expectations.

Nit

It's the tiny things that bug people.

Ostrich

Never bury your head in the sand.

Pig and parrot

Mimicking the words or actions of others won't keep your customers happy.

Quokka

Beware of the unknown international competitor.

Rabbit

Say 'yes' and your success breeds success.

Seal and starfish

Achieve balance between the environment, economics and ethics.

Tiger

Replace the quick sales kill with long-term habits in your habitat.

Unicorn

Get pointed in the right direction.

Vulture

Beware of competition circling.

Whale

Find, train, and keep big performers.

X-breed

Take the best of the best.

Yak

Realise that the perfect organisation is a myth.

Zebra

Be adaptable—it's not all black and white out there.

Going international

The CEO took Phil aside. 'At first I thought you'd gone crazy but you've done great things with your zoo service strategy over the last six months, I just wanted you to know that.' Phil a felt a secret surge of pride at the praise. 'And because it's gone so well we've submitted your work to the industry conference in Tokyo.' Phil was becoming a little concerned. The CEO smiled: 'So I'm sure you're really happy to know you're the keynote speaker at the annual international conference!'

'So that's it', thought Phil. 'I thought it was something I should worry about.' He set it on the back burner and forgot about it. As the time drew closer, Phil's response started to change. Worry wasn't the word. He was terrified at the prospect of speaking in front of an audience of complete strangers—complete strangers who were at the top of the biggest companies in the world.

'I haven't had nearly enough time to work on this presentation', he lamented to Karen, as he was about to leave for the airport. 'I've been too busy actually doing the things we developed after that day at the zoo.'

'Don't worry, dear. They wouldn't have asked you if they hadn't thought you had something worthwhile to say.'

Walking up to the stage 24 hours later, Phil felt his confidence wane. 'If I'm so sure this zoo strategy works, why are my palms sweaty?' he thought. But he was past the point of no return. Taking a deep breath he began speaking, and as he spoke his enthusiasm for what he'd done seemed to take over. Much to his amazement, he started to forget most of his self-consciousness. Noting that the audience was actually listening and nodding knowingly, he continued to share not only his thoughts on the customer service zoo strategy but some of the early successes they'd already had with the implementation.

'At Candon, the key change in six months is that management has accepted that service also depends on them', Phil said. 'Because we haven't swamped people with business jargon, they've taken it on with little resistance and are really running with it. We support them when they get out and talk to customers, we give them the funds and the training support to help staff be autonomous, so they feel head office is with them. With that, staff are beginning to take on responsibility for service levels. The zoo analogy has also simplified frontline training, because the model is really simple, and staff quickly pick up on the metaphor. We even have cartoons, awards and badges based on the animal analogies!'

'One of the key things this process revealed was the power of brainstorming. I've shared how I put it together one day at the zoo . . . but in the following months my team, and the people around them, kept coming up with brilliant additions and variations that helped make the strategy work. More than anything else, the success of this strategy has taught me that brainstorming with an open mind can reveal more than you imagine.'

'But the most surprising part of the program is the way people have made care a part of their business life. Part of the strategy is putting care for yourself, your family and your health right in the middle of the service strategy. It's about people, and it's about heart. It's about connecting the heart and the head. It's enlightened self-interest. If Candon as a business can't look after its own people, how can it look after customers?' Phil spoke easily, setting out the whole range of small successes the strategy had brought.

After the applause had died down and the conference had broken for coffee, Phil noticed a
familiar white-haired man heading his way. As the
man introduced himself, much to his surprise Phil
realised that he had sat next to him on a plane
many months earlier.

Extending his hand, the distinguished gentleman said: 'You may not remember me, but I was
impressed by your lateral thinking at 30 000 feet.'

Remember him? How could Phil forget! This
was the stranger who, through his open-minded
listening, had initially encouraged Phil to think
that his ideas on customer service weren't so crazy
after all. He continued: 'If you're free, I'd like to
chat to you about coming along and talking to our
customer service managers about your ideas. I
think they'll make a huge difference to my company.'

'Your company?' Phil asked.

'Sure, we're one of the largest manufacturers in
the US.'

How could Phil refuse? Candon could afford a
couple more days without him. In fact, he was
beginning to wonder whether it wasn't time that
Candon move into customer service consulting . . .

Customer service . . . Yes, it is a zoo out there.
But it doesn't need to be!

Endnotes

1   Jan Carlzon, *Moments of Truth*, Ballinger, New York, 1987

2   AMR Quantum, 'Customer Satisfaction Australia', Melbourne, March 1993.

3   Karl Albrecht, *The Service Advantage*, Dow Jones, New York, 1990, p. 199.

4   James Belasco, *Teaching the Elephant to Dance*, Hutchinson, UK, 1990.

5   Albrecht, op. cit., p. 199.

6   Ron Zemke and Dick Schaaf, *Service Edge*, New American Library, New York, 1989.

7   Joan Koob Cannie with Donald Caplin, *Customers for Life*, AMACOM, 1991.

125

Bibliography

Albrecht, Karl and Ron Zemke, 1985, *Service America*, Dow Jones-Irwin, Homewood, Illinois

Barker, Joel, 1989, *Discovering the Future*, ILI Press, St Paul, Minnesota

Belasco, James A., 1990, *Teaching the Elephant to Dance*, Hutchinson, UK

Blanchard, Ken with William Oncken Jnr and Hal Burrows, 1989, *The One Minute Manager Meets the Monkey*, Business Library, Melbourne

Carlzon, Jan, 1987, *Moments of Truth*, Ballinger, New York

DeVrye, Catherine, 1994, *Good Service is Good Business*, Prentice-Hall, Sydney

Glasser, Connie, 1995, *Swim with the Dolphins*, Warner, New York

Lynch, Dudley and Paul L. Kordis, 1988, *Strategy of the Dolphin*, William Morris, New York

Mackay, Harvey, 1988, *Swim with the Sharks*, Morrow, New York

Senge, Peter, 1990, *The Fifth Discipline*, Random House, New York

A message from the author

Thank you for reading *The Customer Service Zoo*; we hope you found it helpful.

The Customer Service Zoo was written in response to feedback from tailored, keynote conference sessions, with participants continually looking for material to help them reinforce customer service ideas in their organisations.

Please contact us with any comments, or if you'd like to order or find out more about our range of training materials, or order a customised program for your specific customer service challenges.

CDV Management
Suite 42/20 Bonner Avenue
Manly NSW 2095
Australia

Ph: 61 2 9977 3177
Fax: 61 2 9977 3122
www.cdv.net.au
cdv@ozemail.com.au

Good Service is Good Business: 7 Simple Strategies for Success
One of Australia's best-selling business books, filled with practical examples and case studies.

Good Service is Good Business: complete training kit
Easy-to-use training kit includes a 60-minute staff training video to be used in conjunction with the book and two audio cassettes to reinforce the service message in a time-efficient way.

Good Service is Good Business: audio tapes
One tape contains excerpts from a humorous, live presentation and the other compiles the best of the author's popular radio drive-time series.

Japan: An A–Z Guide of Living and Working in Japan
Contains practical suggestions for those travelling to Japan and working with Japanese companies.